THE ENDURANCE OF SPEED

The Revolutionary New Way to Train for Marathons & Half-Marathons

JASON R. KARP, PhD, MBA

Copyright © 2023 Jason R. Karp

All rights reserved. No part of this book may be reproduced in any form or by any electronic, mechanical, or other means, now known or hereafter invented, including xerography, photocopying, and recording, and in any information storage and retrieval system without the written permission of the author or publisher.

Books are available at special discounts for bulk purchases, including corporate promotions, fundraising, or educational purposes. For discounts or additional permissions: Jason@DrJasonKarp.com.

Notice: The author and publisher specifically disclaim all responsibility for any injury, liability, loss, or risk, personal or otherwise, that is incurred as a consequence, directly or indirectly, of the use and application of any of the contents of this book. Before starting any exercise program, please obtain the approval from a qualified medical professional.

ISBN: 979-8-3720-1578-4
Library of Congress Control Number: 2023902913
Published by Dr. Jason Karp

Cover photo by Enock Kirop, Kimesh Pictures
Cover design by Pixel Studios
Edited by Kathryn F. Galán, Wynnpix Productions

ALSO BY JASON KARP

Coaching the Kenyans

Work Out

Running Periodization

Track & Field Omnibook (ed.)

The Inner Runner

Running a Marathon For Dummies

Lose It Forever

Running for Women

Run Your Fat Off

Sexercise

14-Minute Metabolic Workouts

101 Winning Racing Strategies for Runners

101 Developmental Concepts & Workouts for Cross Country Runners

How to Survive Your PhD

*To my parents,
Muriel and Monroe,
who gave me the intensity for speed and the
persistence for endurance*

CONTENTS

ACKNOWLEDGMENTS	ix
WARM-UP	1
WHAT IS SPEED?	8
WHY SPEED FIRST?	17
THE ENDURANCE OF SPEED	37
THE ENDURANCE OF SPEED TRAINING PROGRAM	63
THE ENDURANCE OF SPEED WORKOUTS	76
COOL-DOWN	86
ENDNOTES	88
ABOUT THE AUTHOR	93

ACKNOWLEDGMENTS

AS I CLOSE THE cover on my fourteenth book, there are several people to thank. Primary among them are all the marathon runners I have coached over the years, including the Kenyan runners in my training group in Kenya and all the other marathon runners I have known, who, collectively, inspired the idea for this book.

Thank you to my literary agent, Grace Freedson. If not for her, publishers may never have read my book proposals. It has been fifteen years since receiving her typewritten letter in my mailbox in my self-addressed stamped envelope, in which she offered to represent me and my work. It was the only piece of mail I received that day, on my final day of receiving mail before moving to another part of the country. I thank her for taking a risk on this nascent author. Fourteen books later, the risk seems to have paid off.

Thank you to Kathryn Galán for her editorial expertise on the first draft of the manuscript. The book is better because of it.

Thank you to the talented photographer, Enock Kirop, for the beautiful photo he took of me running on the dirt track in Kenya, overlooking the Great Rift Valley, that serves as the book's cover photo.

Thank you to my twin brother and playwright, Jack Karp, the best writer I know, who inspires me every day to view writing as art and to work at the craft until I get it right, even if I never get it right.

And thank you to my scientist friends and colleagues, whose research, combined with my academic background and coaching experience at various levels of the sport, has shaped how I think about the physiology of endurance training and enables me to develop my training ideologies.

WARM-UP

I WAS SITTING AT the outdoor patio at the local coffee shop with my chai tea latte when Sara approached me after her sixteen-mile run.

Her black hair was tied back in a ponytail that swayed side to side in the warm breeze. She was still wearing her running shoes, a habit I myself have never adopted, always taking my sweaty shoes off as soon as my run is completed.

She stopped about twenty feet away from me and half-smiled, as if she were anxious about our meeting. She motioned to the door to let me know she was going inside to get something to drink. I nodded.

Sara had run six marathons, her fastest being 3:42. She had also run a couple of ultramarathons—a 50-miler and a 100K. Her goal was to qualify for the Boston Marathon.

Although she was running a lot, things weren't going as well as Sara had hoped. She wasn't living up to her expectations. She was struggling, physically and psychologically. Her training had become work. The training she used to love to do more than anything else. The training that had brought her joy.

A couple minutes later, she came outside, a blended chocolate-chip iced coffee drink wrapped like a present inside her small hands. She sat down to talk about her training and the plan to qualify for Boston. A slight breeze rose, wafting the smell of mocha from inside the coffee shop.

"Looks like a great recovery drink," I said, winking. Sara knew about my research on chocolate milk for post-workout recovery.

"Indeed!" Sara said.

"How was your run?" I asked.

"Good, but I feel slow."

I nodded.

"I want to qualify for Boston," Sara continued. "It's my dream. But I feel like I am far away."

"That's a great goal. Let's see how we can do this. Your Boston Marathon qualifying time of 3:35 is faster than your current lactate threshold pace. But it's not possible to run a marathon faster than threshold pace," I explained. "Given where you are now and the fitness it would take to qualify for Boston, you need to become a faster runner, first."

I gave Sara my honest advice, even though I knew it may be hard for her to hear. No runner wants to be told that he or she is not fast enough to meet his or her goal.

Sara paused. "Okay," she said, looking away as if to avoid eye contact. "We'll do it your way."

Over the next year, Sara agreed to take time away from running marathons, and the long training runs that go with it, and focus on becoming a faster runner. It wasn't easy to convince her; she was a common victim to the allure of the marathon and its endurance training, which attracts so many runners who enter the sport as adults, many of whom seem to think someone is not a runner unless he or she runs marathons. Humans do indeed like to push the limits of endurance, perhaps because, when we push the limits of our endurance, we find out how much we can endure. Our endurance is one of the defining characteristics that make us human. And so, I completely understood where Sara was coming from.

The idea for this book was borne out of my experience coaching Sara and other runners like her.

At first glance, the notion of speed training for a marathon is ridiculous. Who has not experienced that running more miles, even when those miles are run slowly, leads to a faster marathon? The concept of speed seems so contradictory to the long haul of the marathon as to deserve little interest. Ironically, it is just this contradiction that demands that the concept be considered. Because it is often in the contradiction—in doing things differently than how you are used to—that breakthroughs occur.

The book *How to Think Like Einstein* by Scott Thorpe is one of my favorites. It explains that we need to break rules to solve problems and find answers to difficult questions. Little did the author know he was also revealing the secret to running a faster marathon. According to the book, Albert Einstein discovered the theory of relativity by breaking rules that other scientists were unable to break because their preconceived ideas got in the way. They saw things the way they were convinced things were, not the way things could be. Einstein imagined what would happen if the universe acted differently, and he was able to break the rules.

Many new adult runners see the marathon and only the marathon. And so, they train for a marathon almost immediately after starting to run, then train for another one and then another, piling on the miles and running long and slow every weekend, once in a while throwing in a tempo run at a faster, but still aerobic, pace. As the weeks pass and the marathon approaches, they sometimes throw in a few interval workouts of half-mile or one-mile reps or something similar, perhaps with a local running club or with a couple friends training for the same goal or even by themselves.

But they neglect their basic speed.

And they wonder why they can't run a marathon as fast as they want.

It is true that humans are physically engineered more for endurance than for speed. When we compare humans' maximum speed to that of other animals, the result is embarrassing. Humans are rather poor sprinters, with the fastest human able to achieve a maximum speed of only 23.4 miles per hour (Usain Bolt's 100-meter world record of 9.58 seconds). By contrast, the fastest mammal—the cheetah—can run at nearly seventy miles per hour.[1] Even the average house cat, who sleeps curled up in the fetal position most of the day, can run up to thirty miles per hour—with no sprint training, no stretching or foam rolling, no strength training, and no carb loading.

You may be thinking, "Of course cheetahs and other animals can run faster—they have four legs!" But whether an animal has two legs, four legs, or a thousand legs doesn't impact speed. What makes the difference in speed between species and within the human species is not how many legs the animal has or how fast the animal can move its legs, but how much muscular force is applied to the ground with each step. Indeed, how much force you deliver into the ground is the biggest factor that determines your speed, regardless of the distance you're running.

While humans cannot outrun a cheetah or even a house cat, humans are among the best long-distance runners. Our ability to run long distances—and run down faster but less-enduring animals to death—enabled our early ancestors to provide food for their families and thrive as a species.

But running long distances without being fast has its challenges and its limitations.

Speed affects performance for every race distance, from the obvious distance of a 100-meter sprint to the not-so-obvious distance of a marathon. But even a long-distance race like a marathon still requires speed (or at least a reserve of speed), if you want to be good at it. Indeed, if you can't run under nineteen minutes for 5K, you're not going to be able to run under three hours for a marathon.

The Endurance of Speed will help you achieve that, or whatever your marathon goal may be. It is a revolutionary new method of marathon training, arising from two questions: What happens if runners turn the traditional model of distance-running training—establishing aerobic endurance first and then putting speed on top of the aerobic base—on its head and train speed first before training endurance? What happens when runners train at the right speed rather than at the right distance? In *The Endurance of Speed*, you'll discover the remarkable answers to these questions, as you learn how to train your speed first and then learn how to endure a high fraction of that speed.

The training strategy in this book is not for marathon runners who want only to complete a marathon regardless of the time, or runners who have some natural speed and already have a background of speed training (perhaps as a high school or college runner or as an adult runner who is moving up in distance to the marathon after years of racing shorter distances); it's for marathon runners who do not have some natural speed and who do not have a background of speed training, who are frustrated about not getting much better, who are having trouble meeting their goals—like Sara's, qualifying for the Boston Marathon—and who want to run a marathon as fast as possible, regardless of their running level. Elite and sub-elite marathon runners who are already fast runners can also benefit from the strategy in this book, as the Endurance of Speed method builds on the initial development and foundation of speed, extending the duration at which that speed can be sustained as the athletes get closer to the marathon.

What if you broke the rules of your training? What would happen if you trained differently than how you have trained before and took a speed-first approach? What if you first focused on becoming a faster runner and then focused on your endurance of speed? How much faster could you run a marathon or half-marathon?

A speed-first method of training may run counter to what you have been told or read. It's not the typical advice. People often get stuck doing things one way. But the act of training for a marathon can be complicated. Thinking it's complicated means you're learning. Expertise is the foundation of all creative work.

Training for a marathon or half-marathon can indeed be complicated. But it can also be simple. To steal a quip from the New York Yankees' Hall of Fame catcher Yogi Berra, who was asked to explain jazz music, anyone who understands training knows that you can't understand it. It's too complicated. That's what's so simple about it.

And what follows on these pages is going to be simpler—and more effective—than you think.

I hope this book stimulates your curiosity about training, encourages you to break conventional rules, and helps you focus your training on the endurance of speed so that, when you step to the start line of your next marathon or half-marathon, you are ready for the magic.

WHAT IS SPEED?

SPEED ['SPĒD]
NOUN: THE ACT OR STATE OF MOVING SWIFTLY.
VERB: TO MOVE, WORK, OR TAKE PLACE FASTER.

MY OBSESSION WITH running speed started during the Presidential Physical Fitness Tests in fifth grade. Two of the tests were the 50-yard sprint, which we ran in the school's parking lot, and a 600-yard run, which we ran around the grass soccer field. I ran the former in 7.3 seconds and the latter in two minutes and one second. It was then that I discovered I had some talent, although I wasn't the fastest in my class. But I was close. It was also then that I discovered the freedom running confers. Little did I know how much it would change and even direct my life.

A year later, during my first formal race of 400 meters on my middle-school track team, I became hooked. Running as fast as my legs could, I was free.

Free from the noise of the outside world.

Free from the insecurities of my inside self.

And there was no turning back. Thirty-nine years later, I'm still running six days per week, still running to free myself from the noise and the insecurities.

I am not alone. Tens of millions of people run, because runners are who we are. We run because we are animals, and that's what animals evolved to do. Running is essential to an animal's life. Animals run to hunt; they run because they're being hunted; they run to play; they run out of panic; and they even run to flirt with and show off to other members of their species. On school playgrounds across the U.S. and around the world, human animals also show off their speed, as boys and girls race one another during recess.

Over the years, I gravitated to longer distances than the 50-yard and 600-yard tests of the Presidential Physical Fitness Tests. I have run a couple marathons, have coached many marathon runners at many different levels of the sport, and even had the opportunity to author *Running a Marathon For Dummies* for the *For Dummies* book brand. But, through all these experiences, I never lost my fascination with speed and what it can do for distance runners.

What is speed?

It depends who you ask.

If you were to ask George and Charles Merriam and Noah Webster to define speed, they would likely quote their famous dictionary and say that speed, when defined as a noun, is the act or state of moving swiftly; the rate of motion; the magnitude of velocity irrespective of direction; and the swiftness or rate of performance or action. They would go on to say that speed, when defined as a verb, is to make haste; to move, work, or take place faster; and to cause to move quickly.

If you were to ask a physicist to define speed, he or she would say that speed is the rate of change in distance. In other words, how quickly the distance of a moving object changes. Mathematically, speed equals distance divided by time. The physicist would write the equation on the blackboard:

$$\text{Speed} = \frac{\text{Distance}}{\text{Time}}$$

If you want to know what your speed is, the physicist would elaborate, divide the distance you run by the time it took you to run that distance. For example, if you run 10 miles in 90 minutes, your speed is 10 miles divided by 90 minutes, which equals 0.111 mile per minute.

Now, that doesn't make much sense to runners (unless you're a physicist), so we need to multiply that number by 60 minutes (because there's 60 minutes in one hour): 0.111 x 60 = 6.66 miles per hour. That makes more sense, but only if you're running on a treadmill. If you want to know the *pace* you're running instead of the speed, divide the time by the distance: 90 minutes divided by 10 miles = 9 minutes per mile. Easy-peasy! Seems that physics isn't that hard, after all!

If you were to ask a biomechanist to define speed, he or she would say that speed is the product of the distance covered with each step, called *stride length*, and the number of steps taken per minute, called *stride rate*, and then, like the physicist, would write the equation on the blackboard:

$$\text{Speed} = \text{Stride Length} \times \text{Stride Rate}$$

The stride length is typically measured as meters per step, and the stride rate is typically measured as the number of steps per minute. Multiplying those together gives us speed as meters per minute, which can easily be converted into miles per hour or minutes per mile.

What's a little more complicated is what causes a specific stride rate or stride length to occur while you run and what causes them to change.

Stride rate, also referred to as *stride frequency* or *cadence*, is influenced by the central nervous system's ability to recruit muscle fibers to move the legs, the number of fast-twitch muscle fibers, and the metabolic cost of moving the legs. To improve stride rate, you need to improve sprint technique and the quickness of moving your legs. Sprinting, running fast downhill, and running with a metronome set to a higher cadence than what you are used to running at are perhaps the simplest ways to increase stride rate.

Runners tend to subconsciously manipulate stride rate at a given speed and across many speeds based on the minimization of the metabolic cost (i.e., they run at a stride rate that is most economical without even thinking about it). Although there is some individual variation in stride rate between runners, optimal stride rate—the stride rate at which metabolic cost is minimized—seems to be 170 to 180 steps per minute (85 to 90 steps per minute with each leg),[2] with each runner having his or her own most economical stride rate.

Stride length is influenced by the range of motion at the hip—hip extension and hip flexion—and, more importantly, the amount of force the leg muscles drive into the ground. To improve stride length, you need to improve sprint technique and leg muscle strength and power. The physicist would chime in the conversation with the biomechanist (they are related, after all) and say, as Isaac Newton taught in his third law of motion, for every action there is an equal and opposite reaction. Therefore, the more force applied to the ground, the more the runner is projected forward with each step and the longer the stride length.

While it may seem logical that someone who is tall with long legs would take longer strides, making him or her a faster runner, little correlation exists between a person's height and stride length or between a person's leg length and stride length. Taller runners don't take longer strides than shorter runners do. Surprising, huh? The best distance runners in the world (and their legs) are shorter than the population average.

To increase speed, the biomechanist would say, either the stride length or the stride rate or both must increase. However, there's a slight problem, because stride length and stride rate are inversely proportional—as one increases, the other decreases—which means running speed can only increase if an increase in stride length does not occur at the expense of a similar decrease in stride rate or vice versa.

Although much attention is given to stride rate by the popular media, stride length is actually more important for increasing speed in distance runners, once stride rate is in the range of 170 to 180 steps per minute. (If stride rate is less than 170 to 180 steps per minute, training to increase stride rate is beneficial.) When running speed increases from a jog to a run to a fast run, stride length increases more than does stride rate, until the runner is sprinting very fast, at which point stride rate begins to dominate further increases in speed.

Indeed, up to about 3:50 per mile pace, running speed is increased by increasing stride length by the plantar flexor muscles (gastrocnemius and soleus) producing more force against the ground. At very fast speeds (faster than about 3:50 per mile pace), the speed of muscle contraction is so fast that there is not enough time to produce a lot of force, and plantar flexor peak muscle force begins to decrease. The primary (subconscious) strategy used to increase running speed faster than about 3:50 per mile pace shifts from increasing stride length to increasing stride rate. Specifically, the hip muscles (gluteus maximus, psoas, and hamstrings) become prominent players to quickly accelerate the leg forward during the swing phase of the running stride.

Interestingly, the manipulation of stride length and stride rate at different speeds is subconscious, governed by the runner's anatomy and what is most economical for runners; that is, at each speed someone runs, he or she may have a stride length that's most economical (optimizes oxygen use) for him or her to use, while using a specific stride rate (or a narrow range of stride rates) may be what's most economical for *all* distance running speeds. It's a more economical strategy to increase the distance of each stride than it is to increase the cadence of the legs. (Same is true for swimming and rowing—distance per stroke has a greater effect on speed than does the number of strokes per minute.) When sprinting, however, optimizing running economy is not an issue—because sprinting is not about using oxygen—and stride rate can play a more prominent role.

While Merriam-Webster, the physicist, and the biomechanist all have great definitions of speed that help us to understand what speed is, what actually makes a runner get from the start line to the finish line faster?

To answer that question, we must consult an exercise physiologist.

If you were to ask an exercise physiologist to define speed, he or she would say speed is the result of a beautiful integration of anatomical, cardiovascular, muscular, metabolic, and neurological factors that operate cooperatively to influence the production of energy. Together, those factors determine how fast you can run, and those factors are different depending on the distance you're running.

For shorter distances, like 100, 200, and 400 meters, the physiologist would say the factors are mostly anaerobic, which means your muscles don't use oxygen, instead relying on the two anaerobic metabolic pathways to generate the energy needed to run fast. For longer distances, like 3.1 miles (5K), 6.2 miles (10K), 13.1 miles (21.1K), and 26.2 miles (42.2K), the factors are mostly aerobic, which means your muscles use oxygen, relying on the cardiovascular system's ability to deliver oxygen to the muscles and the muscles' ability to use the available oxygen to generate the energy to run. The physiologist would mention fancy terms like VO_2max, the speed at your lactate threshold, running economy, and, to a lesser degree, anaerobic capacity, and further discuss the many variables that influence the transportation of oxygen, the muscles' extraction and use of that oxygen, and the use of the muscle fuels of fat and carbohydrates.

The physiologist, together with the biomechanist and the physicist, would say your running speed is ultimately determined by the speed at which your muscle fibers contract, with the speed limit set by how much and how quickly your legs can apply force to the ground.

Force, and the rate at which that force is applied (called *power*), are influenced by several factors, including neuromuscular coordination (the ability of and speed with which your central nervous system recruits muscle fibers), skeletal muscle mechanics and energetics, efficiency of converting metabolic power into mechanical power, and the aerobic and anaerobic metabolic capacities of skeletal muscle. That's a lot of things to keep track of and try to improve through training, all of which ultimately lead to greater forces in less time being applied to the ground in an efficient, energy-saving manner that projects you forward with each step.

I took a sip of my chai tea latte, which still felt hot to my tongue. "Sara," I said with encouragement, "every runner runs. And every runner runs slowly most of the time. But it takes more than running slowly to be a better runner. It takes more than running slowly to be the best runner you can be.

"Speed is very important for all runners, from 100-meter sprinters to marathon runners and every runner in between, including you. It is only when speed, and the endurance of speed, are neglected that the runner stunts his or her performance potential.

"Don't be that runner.

"Look at your running from the perspective of a strategist. Look at where you are now and where you want to go, and ask yourself, 'Do I have the basic speed to be able to meet my marathon goal? Or do I need to get faster, first?'

"Think of a successful company. The workers of the company don't just do mindless work. They have a manager who strategizes about what's right for the company, how to make the company successful. The manager directs the workers to do the right work that is aligned with the company's mission to get results. That's what you need to do. And you can do it.

"You can qualify for Boston, Sara. You just need to know how to do it.

"The journey starts with speed."

Since she hadn't bolted from the table yet, I added, "Why don't we take a look at how to plan your training differently? It's time to learn about marathon running all over again."

WHY SPEED FIRST?

TO BECOME A FASTER RUNNER, START BY RUNNING FASTER.

IF YOU DELVE INTO the backgrounds of elite marathon runners, you'll find out that nearly all of them were once fast track athletes—in high school, college, and as professional athletes—before they moved up to the marathon distance and became marathon runners. You'll also find out that, once they became marathon runners, they stuck with the marathon and only the marathon; they never went back to the shorter races on the track. Very few elite marathoners began their running careers with the marathon, and practically no elite runners have moved *down* to the marathon from ultramarathons, from the marathon *down* to 5K, or from 5K *down* to the mile/1,500 meters. The strong trend—so strong it is more like an informal law of training and racing—is always to move *up* in distance.

Why?

That's a great question.

And I don't know the complete answer.

What I do know is that the skill of running fast for a short period of time (seconds) is harder and less trainable than the skill of running slower for a long period of time (minutes to hours). With training, it's much easier to become a good marathon runner than it is to become a good sprinter. The old adage that track coaches often live by—"Sprinters are born, while distance runners are made"—also has ample scientific support.[3] This adage implies, of course, that speed is largely about talent, and endurance is largely about training. The truth is both speed and endurance have large genetic underpinnings, and both speed and endurance are trainable; however, endurance is *more* trainable than is speed, which is perhaps exemplified by the millions of people around the world who get off their couch to train for marathons. It's really not that hard to run a marathon, if you train for it.

But it is hard to run a *fast* marathon.

The skill of running fast for a short period of time also is more transient than the skill of running slower for a long period of time. We lose speed rather quickly as we age past our twenties and thirties, but we can hang on to endurance for many years, even decades. That's why elite runners tend to move up in distance when they are not competitive enough on the track in shorter races like 5K and 10K or when they no longer can run as fast as they used to run on the track. When those elite 5K/10K runners move up to the marathon while they are still at or very close to their peak at 5K/10K, that's when they run very fast marathons and half-marathons (and when the world records are broken). On the rare occasions that an elite runner has tried to race a 5K or 10K on the track after having committed to racing marathons, he or she has not been as successful as before making the move up in race distance.

Why speed is less trainable and more transient compared to endurance likely has something to do with the characteristics and trainability of fast-twitch compared to slow-twitch muscle fibers and the limited capacity of anaerobic compared to aerobic metabolism, the details of which are not entirely clear. Whatever the precise physiological reason for not being able to successfully move down in distance, whether from the marathon to the 5K/10K or from the 5K to the mile/1,500 meters, once the commitment is made and the training is undertaken for longer distance races, one thing is clear: to run a marathon as fast as possible, runners need speed as well as endurance. All other factors being equal, a distance runner who is faster for 5K or one mile (or even as short as 50 meters) has the potential to be a better marathon runner compared to a runner who is slower at those shorter races.

Interestingly, several research studies have found sprinting and distance running performance to be significantly correlated, including between a 300-meter sprint time and a 10K run time,[4] between 100-meter and 400-meter sprint times and 5K and 10K run times,[5] and even between a 50-meter sprint time and a 10K run time.[6] Among athletes whose 10K times ranged from 27:29 to 29:06, a 400-meter sprint time explained 72% of the variance in 10K time between runners,[7] and, among thirty-six runners whose 10K times ranged from 32:37 to 56:21, a 300-meter sprint time explained 62% of the variance in 10K time between runners.[8]

Even as far back as the 1960s and 1970s, it was observed that the distance runners who are faster over the shortest distances are also faster at longer distances, even as long as ultramarathons.[9,10] It seems, if you want to find out which runners in your local running group are the fastest in a marathon, you may only need to race them over 400 meters.

The factors that determine peak muscle power production in short-duration, high-intensity exercise, such as racing 800 to 1,500 meters, may also determine performance in more prolonged exercise, including marathon and ultramarathon running, with the factors limiting maximal exercise performance explained in terms of failure of muscle to forcefully contract (i.e., muscle power).[11,12] The historical focus of the field of exercise physiology on only aerobic factors of exercise performance has caught the attention of a few rebellious scientists, including notable physiologist Timothy Noakes, MD, who claimed thirty-five years ago that "the belief that oxygen delivery alone limits maximal exercise performance has straightjacketed exercise physiology for the past thirty years."[13]

The common finding, that how fast people can sprint a short distance (such as 400 meters) as well as other measures of anaerobic power (such as jump height and distance) explains considerable variance in how fast they can run a 10K or a marathon, clearly suggests some common shared physiological mechanism between sprinting and distance running, between anaerobic power and aerobic endurance. It's possible that sprint training results in lower levels of force production relative to one's max when running longer distances, thereby delaying the recruitment of fast-twitch muscle fibers and thus giving the runner greater fatigue resistance.

Although the observation that being faster at short distances equates to being faster at long distances is not new, it has not become the mainstream way of thinking, and, as a result, marathon runners and coaches almost always neglect it. Recreational marathon runners spend far too much time and effort extending the distances they can aerobically run at the expense of how fast they can run. In a homogeneous group of runners with similar aerobic capabilities, the runner with the best anaerobic system will often be the best runner. Even in a heterogeneous group of runners with dissimilar aerobic capabilities, the runner with the best anaerobic system will still often be the best runner.

The other factor that is often neglected is the aerobic benefit obtained from repeated fast running. In addition to improving speed, fast running, when repeated multiple times within a workout, significantly taxes both anaerobic and aerobic metabolism. As the number of reps of an anaerobic interval workout increases, the muscles' reliance on glycolysis progressively decreases and their reliance on aerobic energy production increases. The longer the workout, the more aerobic endurance plays a role, because the ability to repeat fast sprints over and over again requires endurance.

An interesting result of the aerobic involvement in the repetition of sprints is effects similar to traditional aerobic endurance training, such as the stimulation of the synthesis of mitochondrial oxidative enzymes, the stimulation of the factors involved in synthesizing mitochondria (called *mitochondrial biogenesis*), and the reduction in energy expenditure when running at submaximal intensities.[14, 15] These aerobic benefits of speed training make your aerobic runs feel easier.

Distance runners, from recreational to elite, typically take an endurance-to-speed approach with their training: they first create an aerobic "base" by running many miles at a comfortable, aerobic pace, then transition into more quality aerobic running, followed by intervals for aerobic power (VO$_2$max), with little or no attention paid to anaerobic capacity and anaerobic power (except for elite athletes, who do spend time working on their speed at the end of the training season, as they attempt to reach a performance peak for their most important races). This sequence of training—historically called *linear periodization*—was originally designed for athletes in power sports, including track and field, to improve strength, speed, and power. The original model of linear periodization progressed from general conditioning (volume) to specific skills (intensity), with the highest intensity coming at the end of the training program, immediately prior to the competition.

Distance runners began to adopt linear periodization, in part because of the success of the athletes coached by Arthur Lydiard in New Zealand in the 1950s and 1960s. Lydiard strongly argued that a very large volume of aerobic training should be done before anaerobic training is introduced into a distance runner's program. He thought that anaerobic training, with its metabolic acidosis signature, hurts an athlete's aerobic abilities and should therefore be used only sparingly, for just two to three times per week for a few weeks, to bring an athlete to a performance peak.

While Lydiard may have been ahead of his time in his high-mileage approach to training to make the athlete's aerobic capability as robust as possible, there is no scientific or even empirical evidence indicating the metabolic acidosis that occurs with anaerobic training hurts an athlete's aerobic system. More important, there is no scientific justification for the aerobic endurance-based training approach. The body adapts to the stresses to which it is subjected; there is no scientific evidence that the aerobic and anaerobic stresses to which the body is subjected need to be applied in a specific sequence. It is quite possible and perhaps even necessary for distance runners to train anaerobic speed and aerobic endurance at the same time, or even to train the former before the latter.

While linear periodization seems to work well for runners who either are already fast or have spent their developmental years working on speed (as in the case of runners who started training in high school), it doesn't work as well for adult runners who have never run fast in their lives and go straight to the marathon as soon as they become runners.

Since the introduction of linear periodization as a training model, other models have emerged, including the opposite approach—*reverse linear periodization*—which sequences the training from high intensity/low volume to high volume/low intensity.

Most of the scientific research comparing the different models of periodization has been done on strength training, with only one study comparing linear periodization and reverse linear periodization on the development of muscular strength, which found that linear periodization is more effective than reverse linear periodization.[16] This makes sense, since the most intense training comes last in a linear periodized program, which is compatible with the development of muscular strength.

But what if the specific skill you are most interested in mastering is endurance? Is linear periodization the most effective way to train to improve endurance? Scientists at Arizona State University wanted to find out. They divided sixty male and female college students into three groups of twenty (ten males and ten females) who trained on a leg-extension machine twice per week for fifteen weeks:

(1) a linear periodization group, which did three sets of 25-rep max (the maximum weight that can be lifted twenty-five times) for the first five weeks, three sets of 20-rep max for the next five weeks, and three sets of 15-rep max for the final five weeks;

(2) a reverse linear periodization group, which trained with the opposite pattern—three sets of 15-rep max for the first five weeks, three sets of 20-rep max for the next five weeks, and three sets of 25-rep max for the final five weeks; and

(3) an undulating periodization group, which alternated the three workouts—three sets of 25-rep max, three sets of 20-rep max, three sets of 15-rep max—every training day throughout the fifteen weeks.[17]

Following the training, the linear periodization group increased muscular endurance by 56%, the undulating periodization group increased by 55%, and the reverse linear periodization group increased by 73%. When it came to muscular strength, however, reverse linear periodization fared the worst, with a 5.6% increase, compared to 9.1% for linear periodization and 9.8% for undulating periodization. The scientists concluded, "It is apparent that gradual increases in volume (in a reverse linear fashion) are more effective at eliciting endurance gains than increases in intensity."

As the scientists pointed out, this could be a result of reverse linear periodization using a greater volume than linear or undulating periodization immediately before the test of muscular endurance. Of note is, when strength was the fitness factor being tested rather than endurance, reverse linear periodization was not as effective as linear periodization, which increases intensity closer to the test of muscular strength. Thus, linear and undulating periodization are more effective than reverse linear periodization for increasing muscle strength, while reverse linear periodization is more effective for increasing muscle endurance. Very interesting.

Muscular endurance is one thing; aerobic endurance while running is quite another. When it comes to aerobic endurance performance, there is a lack of scientific evidence on the efficacy of one periodization model over another. Only a few studies have examined the effects of reverse linear periodization on either the physiological factors of running or on actual race (or time trial) performance, with results showing a slight or no superiority of reverse linear periodization.[18, 19, 20, 21]

In one of those studies, thirty male and female recreational runners were randomly assigned to one of three groups that did interval training for twelve weeks:

(1) a linear periodization group, which began the training program with longer interval workouts at a lower intensity and progressed to shorter workouts at a higher intensity,

(2) a reverse linear periodization group, which began the training program with shorter interval workouts at a higher intensity and progressed to longer workouts at a lower intensity, and

(3) a control group, which continued with its own independent training.

Workout paces for the linear and reverse linear periodization groups were based on a 5K time trial at the beginning of the study. After twelve weeks of training, the linear periodization group improved its 5K time trial by an average of 5.5% (1 minute, 17 seconds), the reverse linear periodization group improved by 8.1% (1 minute, 53 seconds), and the control group improved by 0.1% (4 seconds). Both periodization groups had a significantly greater improvement than did the control group, but despite the greater improvement in the reverse linear periodization group, there was no statistical difference between the periodization groups. All three groups slightly improved VO_2max, speed at lactate threshold, and running economy, although there were no differences between groups.

Despite no superiority of one type of periodization over the other in regard to physiological factors and a small practical superiority of the reverse linear periodization on 5K time trial performance, an interesting finding of this study is that the reverse linear periodization group felt that the longer interval workouts (which came later in the training program for reverse linear periodization and earlier for linear periodization) were less demanding (lower rating of perceived exertion scores, in technical language) than the linear periodization group. This suggests that doing faster, anaerobic workouts first can make the later, more metabolically demanding VO_2max workouts seem easier.

In another study at University of Agder in Norway, three different periodization models of interval training were compared for twelve weeks.[22] Sixty-three cyclists were divided into three groups matched for age, cycling experience, body mass, and physiological factors (VO_2max, power output at lactate threshold, peak power output, and average power output during an all-out forty-minute time trial): (1) linear periodization, (2) reverse linear periodization, and (3) undulating periodization.

Each group did eight interval workouts in each of three four-week training cycles. The linear periodization group increased intensity over the twelve weeks, with eight workouts of 4 x 16 minutes in weeks one to four, eight workouts of 4 x 8 minutes in weeks five to eight, and eight workouts of 4 x 4 minutes in weeks nine to twelve; the reverse linear periodization group did the opposite pattern, with eight workouts of 4 x 4 minutes in weeks one to four, eight workouts of 4 x 8 minutes in weeks five to eight, and eight workouts of 4 x 16 minutes in weeks nine to twelve; and the undulating periodization group mixed the intensity over the twelve weeks, alternating workouts of 4 x 16 minutes, 4 x 8 minutes, and 4 x 4 minutes in each four-week training cycle. All workouts were done with two minutes of recovery between reps. All cyclists completed twenty-four interval workouts in twelve weeks. For six weeks prior to the twelve-week training intervention and on non-interval workout days during the intervention, the cyclists did as much low-intensity training as they wanted.

After twelve weeks, all three groups significantly increased power output at lactate threshold (by 3-6%) and both forty-minute time trial power output and peak power output (by 5-8%), although the specific organization of the interval training (linear, reverse linear, undulating) didn't seem to matter, as there were no differences between groups. On an individual basis, however, more people fared better with the linear periodization approach: 87% of participants in the linear periodization group improved forty-minute time trial power output by more than 3%, compared to 63% of participants in the reverse linear periodization group and 56% of participants in the undulating periodization group.

The few other studies that have compared reverse linear periodization to another periodization model have also not shown that reverse linear periodization is a better training method, in part because the studies did not match the participants on physiological variables or time trial performance when separating them into groups, nor did they equate the overall training load between training groups, which makes it difficult to assess the efficacy of one periodization model over another.

While the small amount of research on models of periodization doesn't support reverse linear periodization being better than linear periodization (except in the case of strength training for muscular endurance), it doesn't support its being worse. Reverse linear periodization may be most effective for long-distance races, like marathon and half-marathon, for several reasons.

(1) More marathon-specific work as the race approaches.

Since the half-marathon and marathon depend so heavily on aerobic endurance, a training program that focuses more on endurance as you get closer to the race is more likely to produce better results. Long runs, acidosis (lactate) threshold runs, marathon-pace runs, and higher overall mileage is more marathon- and half-marathon-specific than are VO$_2$max interval workouts. If you use a linear periodized approach for the marathon and half-marathon, that would mean you're reducing the volume while increasing the intensity as you get closer to the race. If you take a reverse linear periodized approach, by starting with higher intensity and decreasing the intensity over time as you increase the volume, you're doing more race-specific work as you get closer to the race.

(2) Increased speed reserve.

Training speed first increases your "speed reserve," which makes marathon goal pace easier. For example, say you have run 3:15 for a marathon (7:26 per mile pace) and your goal is to run 2:59 (6:52 per mile pace). Your one-mile PR is 6:20, which means you ran the marathon one minute and six seconds per mile (or 17.4%) slower than your one-mile time (which is very good). However, with a one-mile PR of 6:20, you won't be able to run 6:52 pace for two hours and 59 minutes; that's a difference in pace of only 32 seconds (or 8.4% slower) per mile. Even if your mile PR is

6:00, you still won't be able to run a marathon in under three hours.

To run a faster marathon, you can continue to drive the endurance nail into the wall with greater and greater amounts of mileage, long runs, and tempo runs to narrow the difference between your marathon pace and your one-mile PR, or you can first work on your basic speed to run one mile faster—giving yourself a bigger speed reserve—and then train your ability to hold a high fraction of that speed. If you can get your one-mile time down to 5:46, which increases your speed reserve, then 6:52 pace is the same pace difference (1:06 per mile; 19.1% slower) as when you ran 3:15.

Many runners want to run a faster marathon or half-marathon, but they don't have the speed reserve to do so. They also lack experience with faster running, instead getting caught up in the long-run, slow-mileage-building approach to marathon training. Many recreational runners, even those who are good, would be well served by developing their speed and becoming faster, more proficient runners before focusing their attention on the marathon.

(3) Increased VO$_2$max after training anaerobic capacity.

The physiological rationale for taking a reverse linear periodization approach for the marathon and half-marathon considers that VO$_2$max should be targeted after improving anaerobic capacity. Even though VO$_2$max is considered an aerobic factor that represents the maximum capability of your cardiovascular system to supply oxygen to the working muscles, it is often unrecognized that the running speed at which VO₂max occurs includes a large dependence on anaerobic metabolism. In other words, when you rev your aerobic engine as fast as it can go, your muscles also rely on anaerobic metabolism to run at that speed.

Research has shown that the amount of time athletes can sustain exercise at VO₂max is positively correlated with their anaerobic capacity (i.e., athletes with a larger anaerobic capacity are able to sustain exercise at VO₂max for a longer time than athletes with a poorer anaerobic capacity),[23] and that sprint-interval training itself improves VO₂max (primarily via muscle fiber recruitment and muscular metabolic mechanisms),[24] supporting the significant role that anaerobic fitness (speed) plays in VO₂max and distance running performances.

Furthermore, the improved anaerobic fitness gained from speed training makes the more metabolically demanding VO₂max workouts seem easier. Jumping into VO₂max workouts without first training speed (translated physiologically as anaerobic power and capacity) makes the already hard VO₂max workouts even harder because of their aerobic and anaerobic metabolic stress.

(4) Larger aerobic engine before engine sustainability.

The physiological rationale also considers that VO₂max should be improved before focusing on improving the fraction of VO₂max that you can sustain, which is reflected by the acidosis (lactate) threshold, as well as other metabolic factors. In other words, build as large of an aerobic engine as possible, and then build your sustainability of the engine—80% of a Ferrari is faster than 80% of a Mitsubishi.

Why all the attention on VO₂max? Why do we care about what training precedes or succeeds VO₂max? Because VO₂max (or, more precisely, the running speed at which VO₂max is reached) is the ultimate ruler of distance-running performance, setting the upper limit for aerobic metabolism. VO₂max explains much of the difference in performance between runners, even between those who are elite and sub-elite.[25] Only in a group of homogeneous runners with similar VO₂max is VO₂max not a good predictor of performance.

If you want to be the best runner you can be, you need to make your VO₂max as high as possible (and increase the speed at which you're running when you're running at VO₂max) and be able to sustain as high of a fraction of your VO₂max as possible (which is reflected by the acidosis threshold and running economy). If you acquire both those traits—a high VO₂max and a high fraction of VO₂max that you can sustain—your marathon (or half-marathon) performance will reach a much higher level.

(5) Improved running economy.

Speed training improves running economy. In 1930, Dr. David Dill and his colleagues at the Harvard Fatigue Laboratory were among the first physiologists to observe that there are marked differences in the amount of oxygen different people use when running at the same submaximal speeds. These differences in what they called "running economy"—the volume of oxygen (VO_2) used to run at submaximal speeds—are a major factor in explaining differences in distance-running performance and why runners with the same VO_2max do not all cross the race finish line at the same time.

For example, when you run at a 10-minute mile or 9-minute mile or 8-minute mile pace, you'll consume a specific amount of oxygen every minute (which gets higher the faster the pace) to maintain each of those speeds. While VO_2max explains what happens at the upper limit of oxygen use, running economy explains what happens at levels below that upper limit. The less oxygen you use to run at a given submaximal speed, the better runner you'll be.

Ample scientific evidence exists that sprint running (e.g., 20 to 100 meters), along with other forms of muscle power training, such as plyometrics, improves running economy.[26, 27, 28, 29, 30] Improving running economy as early as possible in the training program sets you up for all the endurance training to come.

(6) Improved running skill.

The early introduction of speed training can improve running skill, which is especially important for recreational and less-skilled runners. Most people who run just walk out the door and start running. They concern themselves with training-related variables, such as weekly mileage, duration of long runs, pace per mile, and heart rate, and sometimes they give even more concern to the proper angle and lighting of their post-run Instagram photo. They pay little or no attention to *how* they run.

Developing the skill of running is the first (and often neglected) step in becoming a better runner or preparing for a race. That skill is largely attributable to efficient running mechanics, rather than the metabolic and cardiovascular factors of running. Sprinting improves several mechanical and neuromuscular factors, including neuromuscular coordination (the coordinated recruitment of muscle fibers by your central nervous system), ground contact time, and muscles' ability to produce force against the ground, all of which clean up biomechanical flaws and cause less energy to be wasted on braking forces and less vertical oscillation.

With a more proficient running skill, you'll be better able to handle and even thrive off your training. Workouts in subsequent phases of your training will also feel easier and more fluid, as you become a master of the skill of running early in your training journey.

To become a faster runner, start by running faster.

Sara and I were still sitting on the coffee shop patio, sipping our drinks, the palm trees providing shade on this warm day. She was sitting on the edge of her chair with her legs crossed, still wearing her running clothes.

"Wow, I wish I knew all this before," Sara said, twirling the straw of her drink between her fingers. "I want to be a faster marathon runner. What can I do differently now?"

"That's exactly the right question to ask, Sara," I said. "Because it means you are committed.

"There are many physiological and biochemical reasons for how and why you become a better runner, which are all very interesting and knowing them enables you to affect specific outcomes from your training and become more proficient at the task. Becoming good at running—at anything for that matter—requires practice and patience.

"Practice, because it takes repetition of a task to master it.

"Patience, because, when you run, you're trying to change things at the level of the cell, where the business of life occurs, where the nucleic acids and bases exist that make up the helical strands of your DNA. That doesn't happen overnight.

"Most amateur marathon runners begin their training with endurance and try to drive the endurance nail into the wall with greater and greater amounts of mileage, long runs, and tempo runs," I continued. "This strategy can work for a while, as a four-hour marathon runner or a 3:30 marathon runner can improve quite a lot off of purely aerobic training. The problem is that many amateur runners go straight to the marathon without ever having worked on their basic speed, without ever having touched a fast-twitch muscle fiber. At some point, those runners will reach a plateau, always limited by their lack of speed. Their fast-twitch muscle fibers just sit there, wasting away. But the fast-twitch muscle fibers need attention, too. The best marathon runners are fast runners. Not just fast marathon runners, but fast runners.

"You need to touch a fast-twitch fiber, Sara."

Sara chuckled.

"You can acquire that speed. But once you have that speed, Sara, speed alone is not enough.

"The speed-endurance equation works one way but not the other. To run a fast marathon, a runner needs to be fast, but if a runner is fast, that doesn't mean he or she can run a fast marathon. The fast runner still needs to acquire the endurance of speed to run a fast marathon.

"For you to run a marathon in 3:35 and qualify for the Boston Marathon, you need to be able to run 5K in 22:30 and one mile in 6:38. But if you can run 5K in 22:30 and one mile in 6:38, that doesn't mean you'll automatically run a marathon in 3:35, unless you acquire the endurance of speed.

"And so, we have another part of the process to talk about."

THE ENDURANCE OF SPEED

IF I RUN 100 METERS TWENTY TIMES, THAT IS TWO KILOMETERS, AND THAT IS NO LONGER A SPRINT.

I ONCE COACHED a thirty-three-year-old runner who ran a 2:48:39 marathon on 80 to 85 miles per week. Soon after she ran that time, which had just missed the then qualifying time for the U.S. Olympic Marathon Trials by 39 seconds, she joined a sponsored group with a coach, who said to me, "She can run mid-2:30s."

After coaching her in person for two years and seeing what she could do, I was skeptical she could run a marathon in the mid-2:30s, so I just nodded, smiled, and kept my mouth shut. To run a marathon that fast, she would have needed to be able to run 5K in 16:00 to 16:15, and, to do that, she would have needed to be able to run one mile in 4:40 to 4:45. At the time of that conversation with her new coach, her 5K PR was 18:08, after quite a lot of training.

Many years later, I coached another thirty-three-year-old runner who ran a 2:57 marathon, also after a lot of training that touched 100 miles per week. She told me her goal was to run a 2:37 marathon and sub-17-minute 5K, the former being the women's U.S. Olympic Trials qualifying time. Unfortunately, she, too, didn't have the basic speed to run either of those times. To do so, she would need to be able to run one mile in 4:55, and to do that, she would need to be able to run 400 meters in less than 60 seconds.

These runners are not alone. Many runners want to run a marathon (or any distance) significantly faster than they currently do, myself included. Perhaps you're also one of them, which is why you're reading this book. However, to run significantly faster—and take your performance to another level—you must first have some basic speed, and then you must have amazing endurance.

That's what the Endurance of Speed method gives you: a strong foundation of speed, and the technical skill that accompanies it, from which you work on speed endurance and specific endurance to reach a new level of fitness and run a much faster marathon (or half-marathon).

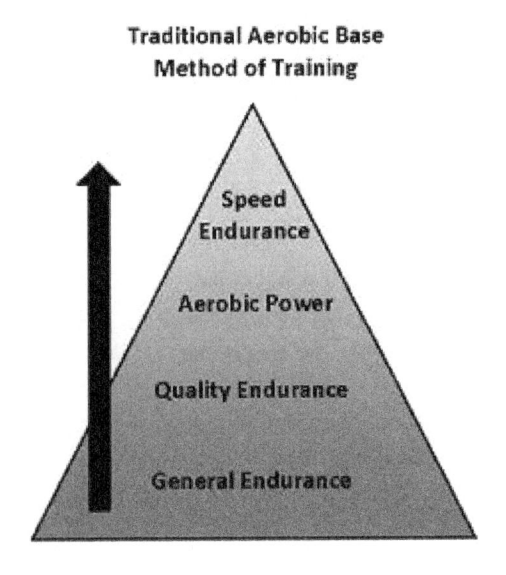

Traditional Aerobic Base Method of Training

- Speed Endurance
- Aerobic Power
- Quality Endurance
- General Endurance

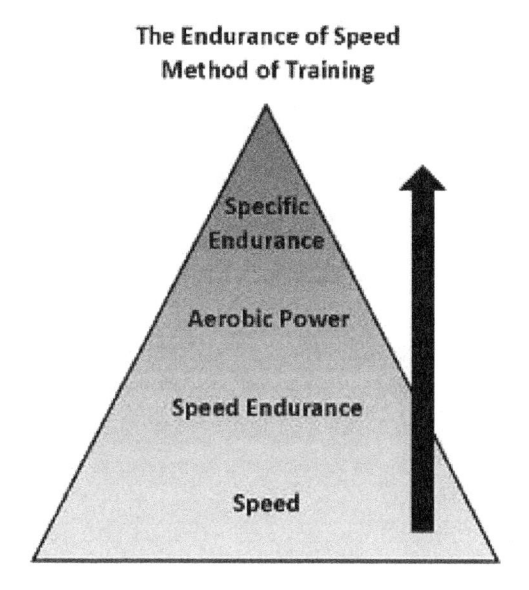

**The Endurance of Speed
Method of Training**

- Specific Endurance
- Aerobic Power
- Speed Endurance
- Speed

The Endurance of Speed method consists of five major themes:

(1) Initial development of basic speed to become a faster runner.

Most marathon training programs you'll find in books or online neglect the development of speed, instead focusing on the weekly mileage and duration of the long run. Most runners and coaches think that sprinting is a waste of time while training for a marathon. They think, because the marathon is 100% aerobic, the training should reflect that and also be 100% aerobic.

Logically, that makes sense. However, if you never devote any training time to sprinting to develop your basic speed, you'll limit how fast your marathon can get. And if you never train your fast-twitch muscle fibers, you can never rely on them for the power they produce or the fuel they store. (Sprint training increases glycogen concentration similarly in all three muscle-fiber types and reduces the rate of glycogen used at submaximal exercise intensities.[31])

When you become a faster runner, your marathon pace will feel easier, and you'll be able to run a faster marathon. 70% of five-minute mile pace is faster than 70% of 5:30 mile pace.

(2) More marathon-specific work as the race approaches.

By starting with higher intensity and then progressing to higher volume, instead of the other way around as is typical of most marathon training programs, you do the most marathon-specific work at the time you need it.

The decrease in intensity with concomitant increase in volume doesn't mean the training gets easier, as one might think it would, since runners often associate intensity with difficulty; only that the later emphasis of the training is on marathon-specific endurance. Accompanying the physical benefit of doing more marathon-specific work as the race approaches are the mental benefit and confidence gained from doing such specific work.

(3) Training at the right speed rather than at the right distance.

The Endurance of Speed method focuses on extending the duration at which you can sustain goal marathon pace rather than focusing on the duration of the long run.

If I were to tell a group of 3:10 marathon runners that their workout today is to run ten miles at six-minute mile pace, most of the runners in the group would be intimidated, and they would either start the run at a pace they thought they could sustain for ten miles, or they would start at six-minute mile pace and adjust the pace as needed to complete ten miles, even if it meant getting considerably slower throughout the run as they fatigue. However, what if they were to start the run at six-minute mile pace and run for as long as they could at that pace, even if they stopped running after five miles?

To most runners, completing the distance is most important. If their marathon training plan calls for twenty miles on Sunday morning, they will run twenty miles, not eighteen miles or nineteen or 19.87, and they will run whatever pace they need to make sure they complete twenty miles. How many times have you run a little more at the end of your run because your GPS watch says you ran 9.92 miles instead of your planned ten?

Unless you're training to *complete* a marathon, with no regard to the amount of time it takes to complete it, or you're a beginner, training for your first or second marathon, there's not much value in running long and easy all the time, since that is not specific training to running a fast marathon.

Running long, slow distances at a pace much slower than the marathon is better than nothing and will certainly improve various physiological factors, including capillarization (the growth and development of new capillaries that deliver oxygen to the muscle fibers), mitochondrial biogenesis (the synthesis of mitochondria), and fat oxidation, but it's not nearly as effective as long, fast distance and will not enable a runner to meet his or her potential in the marathon.

Likewise, running shorter distances at much faster than marathon pace (e.g., interval training) will certainly improve other physiological factors, including cardiac output, oxygen transport, and VO_2max, but does not mean the runner can sustain a pace near his or her acidosis (lactate) threshold for a very long time, as in the case of running a marathon.

One of the biggest mistakes runners and coaches make when training for a marathon is not considering the demands of the race and not being specific enough in their training to meet those demands. Furthermore, many runners misjudge their fitness, thinking they're in better shape than they really are based on a specific workout or a long run they've completed that doesn't correlate to the marathon.

For beginner or recreational marathon runners, much of the training, by necessity, should be general, because a foundation of aerobic fitness needs to be created. After years of running, much more of the marathon runner's training should be specific to the demands of the marathon. Once you are already trained, running long and slow just doesn't cut it anymore. It is much easier to run at 90% of your speed if your baseline running is at 80% than it is if your baseline running is at 60%. It is also much easier to extend the familiar intensity than it is to introduce an unfamiliar intensity.

How you accomplish this is not by increasing the training volume or the intensity from year to year, but by increasing the volume *of* intensity—the volume of specific workouts and the volume of running at marathon pace, with the end goal of sustaining your realistic goal marathon pace for longer and longer periods of time—ideally, for the entire 26.2 miles. This process takes months to years (depending on how aggressive your marathon goal is), not weeks. The Endurance of Speed method is a long-term approach, not a quick fix.

The key word above is *realistic*. A runner's race time goals are often arbitrary and not in agreement with what is realistic. I have coached many runners over the years, including that 2:57 marathoner who wanted to run 2:37, who had unrealistic goals that were not achievable because they didn't have the basic speed.

If the goal race pace is unrealistic, then any workouts at goal race pace will be way over the runner's head, and he or she will risk running himself or herself into the ground, trying to accomplish them. For the Endurance of Speed method to work, your goal needs to be realistic—perhaps five to ten minutes for a recreational to good marathoner, and fewer minutes for an elite marathoner (some marathoners can improve by much more, if their prior marathon(s) was(were) way below their capabilities)—because, if the marathon time you want to run is way over your head, it will be very difficult to keep extending the duration you can sustain goal marathon pace. It's great to have a big goal, but you reach the goal one step at a time.

Even if the runner's goal time is realistic, that goal race pace represents a future level of fitness, not a current one. Doing workouts now at that future fitness level means the runner will be running faster than what he or she needs to run in order to meet the desired purpose, which adds to the training stress. The runner will no longer be training at his or her acidosis threshold pace to train acidosis threshold, or VO_2max pace to train VO_2max.

For example, if that 2:57 marathon runner does her acidosis threshold workouts based on her goal of a 2:37 marathon, her workouts would no longer be purely aerobic; they would become partially anaerobic, which would change the desired purpose and stress of the workouts. Indeed, her goal marathon pace (5:59 per mile) would be faster than her current acidosis threshold pace (6:20-6:25 per mile)! No one, not even the marathon world-record holder, can run a marathon averaging a pace faster than acidosis (lactate) threshold.

Since running at goal race pace (or calculating workout paces based off goal race pace) moves the runner away from targeting the specific physiological factors that dictate running performance, it must be used sparingly, done over a long period of time, and, I recommend, employed only when training for a marathon or half-marathon, which are aerobic in nature.

Performing workouts based on a goal race pace for one mile, 5K, or 10K changes the physiology of the workouts too much, making them much more anaerobic. The anaerobic component inherent in shorter races makes it much more difficult to extend the duration a runner can sustain goal race pace. (Sprinting speeds are much harder to sustain than distance running speeds. For example, there is a greater drop off in speed between racing 100 meters and 400 meters than there is between racing 10K and a marathon, despite the difference in running time between 100 and 400 meters being much less than that between 10K and marathon.) The longer the duration of the effort, the better (and more trainable) the endurance of speed, because of the body's renewable aerobic sources of energy.

For those shorter races, it's more effective to target the specific physiological factors that determine race performance and to run only as fast as needed to meet the purpose of the workouts. The Endurance of Speed method is not a training method meant for shorter races; it's specific to the marathon and half-marathon. That doesn't mean you can't give the Endurance of Speed method a try for shorter races and work on extending the duration you can sustain goal race pace, only that it is much more difficult to do so.

(4) Interval training with unlimited reps.

Last time you did an interval workout, did you have a specific number of reps decided before the workout? Nearly all coaches prescribe and nearly all runners perform a specific number of reps for interval workouts, with that number decided before the workout begins. However, the number of reps is not all that important and is usually an arbitrary decision. There's no magic in doing five or six or ten reps. What is important is causing fatigue during the workout, because fatigue is what your body responds and adapts to.

The number of reps at which you fatigue may change from week to week based on many factors (e.g., the training you did in the days prior to the workout, the amount of sleep you had the night before the workout, the quality and quantity of your nutrition prior to the workout, daily variation in performance, changes in fitness, etc.). You may experience the same amount of fatigue today after eleven reps and next week after nine reps. That's okay. Do as many reps as it takes to cause a sufficient amount of fatigue on that day, until you feel you couldn't do another rep without catastrophic physiological events occurring (in other words, stop the workout before you throw up or collapse from heat exhaustion).

Workouts should not be done to failure, until you're throwing up on the side of the track or road, or until you collapse. But they should cause enough fatigue, enough stress, to which to adapt. You should always walk away from a workout feeling like you're in control of the workout rather than the workout controlling you. You (or your coach) need to assess when you have completed enough reps to reap the reward of the workout.

In addition to the physiological reasons for training with unlimited reps is the psychological reason: to avoid limiting yourself. If you focus on one rep at a time without any preconceived idea as to how many reps you'll do, you're forced to stay in the moment and focus only on the rep you're running. When you do that, you may end up completing the workout running more reps than what you thought you could.

If you decide before the workout that you'll do eight reps, guess what happens when you get to rep seven or eight? You feel tired, because your brain thinks you're close to the end of the workout. Anticipation of an end point affects your feelings of fatigue, your associative thought processes, and even your neuromuscular efficiency. [32] Deciding beforehand (or being told by a coach) how long the workout is going to be also affects your pacing, because optimal pacing strategy is strongly influenced by the duration of exercise.[33]

If you leave the workout open-ended, you'll be surprised at what you can accomplish. The Endurance of Speed method includes interval workouts with unlimited reps to train your endurance of speed and to reset your limits by not placing limits on your workouts... or on yourself.

(5) Interval training with a high volume of reps.

Running many miles or kilometers per week is not the only way to build endurance. It's a great (and necessary) way to build general endurance, but not specific endurance. To build specific endurance—the endurance of speed—you need to run faster paces for longer. And one clever way to do that is to break up your interval workouts into shorter reps so you can do more of them and spend more time per workout at a given intensity.

In a laboratory in Sweden in the 1960s, well-known Swedish physiologist Per-Olof Åstrand discovered, using a stationary bicycle, that by breaking up a set amount of exercise into smaller segments, you can perform a greater volume of work at the same or even higher intensity. For example, you can run more than 5,000 meters at 5,000-meter race pace if you break up the 5,000 meters into 1,000-

meter reps with rest breaks; you can run even more if you break up the 1,000-meter reps into 500-meter reps with rest breaks; and you can run even more if you break up the 500-meter reps into 200-meter reps with rest breaks. The shorter the distance run, the more total distance (and time) you can complete in the workout at the same pace.

The Endurance of Speed method includes high-volume interval workouts to improve your specific endurance. Czechoslovakian distance runner Emil Zátopek, four-time Olympic gold medalist, was on to this endurance-building strategy, as he once responded, when asked why he ran such short distances in training when he was a distance runner, "If I run 100 meters twenty times, that is two kilometers and that is no longer a sprint."

So, let's get to it. The thirty-eight-week training program that follows is divided into three phases: general preparation (sixteen weeks), specific preparation (twenty weeks), and taper (two weeks). A recovery/transition phase of two weeks follows the training, making the entire program forty weeks.

This is longer than most marathon training programs you'll find in other books, online, or from other coaches. That's because of the time the Endurance of Speed method devotes to speed development (subtracting the first phase of sixteen weeks yields a more traditional program of twenty-two weeks). The program begins with high intensity to improve your speed and, over time, decreases in intensity while increasing in both volume and marathon-specific endurance.

The general preparation phase is made up of four training cycles of four weeks each and emphasizes anaerobic power, anaerobic capacity, anaerobic capacity/aerobic power, and aerobic power, respectively. The specific preparation phase is made up of five training cycles of four weeks each, emphasizing aerobic capacity, acidosis threshold, and marathon pace. The latter part of the program includes more race-specific endurance training as you approach your race, to improve your ability to maintain a high fraction of the speed you trained in the general preparation phase.

The program is designed to be flexible to work around your schedule and individual needs. I prescribe the work that needs to be done each week, rather than as a day-by-day calendar, and you choose the specific workouts from the Endurance of Speed Workouts and decide which days of the week to do them. You can also add or subtract weeks, depending on the number of weeks you have until your race.

If you have more than thirty-six weeks for the general and specific preparation phases, you can add extra weeks where you need them most—in the general preparation phase, if you need to work more on your speed; in the specific preparation phase, if you need to work more on endurance; or in both phases. If you have less than thirty-six weeks for the general and specific preparation phases, you can subtract weeks from where you need them least.

PHASE 1: GENERAL PREPARATION (16 weeks)

Phase 1 of the Endurance of Speed training program focuses first on pure speed (anaerobic power) and then on speed endurance (anaerobic capacity), with short and long sprints, respectively. The weekly mileage remains low to moderate, at 55-70% of the planned peak.

To accurately determine your goal marathon pace (or half-marathon pace, if you're training for a half-marathon) for the marathon-specific training that you'll do in Phase 2 of the training program, run a few races during Phase 1. Races, which can serve as a substitute for one of the prescribed workouts, are the best test of your fitness and the most accurate way to predict your time for any other race distance.

Training Cycle 1: Anaerobic Power (4 weeks)

Training begins with anaerobic power (the true speed work), which targets the phosphagen (creatine phosphate) energy system. Anaerobic power is best trained with interval workouts, running very fast sprints for five to twenty seconds, with standing/walking recovery intervals of three to five minutes. The relatively long recovery intervals between sprints enable creatine phosphate to be replenished in the muscles so it can be used as fuel for the next rep.

Given the emphasis on high intensity during this first training cycle, the weekly mileage is only 55% of the planned peak. This gives plenty of room to grow the volume throughout the training program.

Many marathon runners shy away from sprinting, either because they are timid about fast running, they think that sprinting is not part of marathon training, they think sprinting is only for fast runners, or they think sprinting will get them injured. But none of these things are true, and you are not timid. How do you think you become a faster runner? By developing your speed!

Training Cycle 1 also introduces ten- to thirty-second "strides" (short, non-fatiguing bursts of fast running) twice per week after completing an easy run, which continue throughout the entire training program. See The Endurance of Speed Workouts chapter.

Training Cycle 2: Anaerobic Capacity (4 weeks)

Training continues in Training Cycle 2 with anaerobic capacity (speed endurance), accompanied by a slight increase in weekly volume to 60% of the planned peak mileage. Anaerobic capacity targets the metabolic energy system of anaerobic glycolysis (the breakdown of glucose to provide energy). When your running pace exceeds the rate at which your heart and blood flow can provide oxygen to your muscles, anaerobic metabolism kicks into high gear, quickly breaking down glucose to produce energy for your muscles.

Your anaerobic capacity is best trained with interval workouts, running fast for thirty to ninety seconds at a time, with jogging recovery intervals that are at least double the length of time as the reps.

These workouts improve your speed several ways: by increasing the enzymes involved in glycolysis (which makes the chemical reactions occur faster), by improving your ability to buffer muscle acidosis, by enhancing the neural recruitment of muscle fibers, and by training the powerful fast-twitch muscle fibers.

With anaerobic interval training, leave your heart rate monitor at home, since heart rate does not adequately reflect the workout intensity—you'll be running at a pace much faster than that which will elicit max heart rate, although for a shorter time than it takes to reach it. Anaerobic training is not about heart rate and oxygen delivery; it's about the metabolic activity going on inside your skeletal muscles.

Training Cycle 3: Anaerobic Capacity & Aerobic Power (4 weeks)

The training continues with an emphasis on anaerobic capacity, and it introduces aerobic power training, with one workout of each per week. The weekly volume increases slightly, to 65% of the planned peak mileage. Aerobic power refers to VO_2max, which is the maximum volume of oxygen your muscles can consume per minute. Aerobic power training targets your cardiovascular system's ability to pump blood and oxygen to the working muscles.

Aerobic power is best trained with interval workouts, running hard for three to five minutes at or very near your maximum heart rate, with jogging recovery intervals that are slightly less than or equal to the time of the reps. The main reason to jog during the recovery intervals is to increase venous return (the return of blood back to the heart through the venous circulation) via the muscles' pumping action, so the heart can receive and subsequently pump more blood with each beat (stroke volume). Jogging is also important (compared to standing still or walking) to keep oxygen consumption (VO_2) elevated throughout the workout.

VO_2max pace for recreational and intermediate-level runners:

- Between 1.5-mile and 2-mile/3K race pace
- About 20-25 seconds per mile faster than 5K race pace
- About 40-45 seconds per mile faster than 10K race pace
- 95-100% max heart rate

VO_2max pace for competitive and highly trained runners:

- Equal or very close to 2-mile/3K race pace
- About 10-15 seconds per mile faster than 5K race pace
- About 25-30 seconds per mile faster than 10K race pace
- 95-100% max heart rate

To do VO_2max workouts by heart rate, it's important to know what your true max heart rate is. To determine your max heart rate, run one mile—four laps of a standard outdoor track—while wearing a heart rate monitor (with a chest strap), starting at a comfortable pace and picking up the pace each lap until you're running as fast as you can over the final lap. Check the heart rate monitor a few times over the final lap. The highest number you see is your max heart rate.

Training Cycle 4: Aerobic Power (4 weeks)

Training Cycle 4 emphasizes aerobic power, with two workouts per week. As you start to transition to more aerobic training, the weekly mileage continues to slowly increase, reaching 70% of the planned peak.

PHASE 2: SPECIFIC PREPARATION (20 weeks)

Phase 2 of the Endurance of Speed training program focuses on marathon-specific endurance, with longer acidosis threshold workouts and marathon-pace runs. Much of the previous training prepares you for this phase of the training program, as you focus on raising your threshold and sustaining goal marathon pace.

Continuous runs at marathon pace become among the most important training in Phase 2, as the date of the marathon approaches. Accompanying the marathon-specific workouts is a steady increase in the weekly mileage, ranging from 75-100% of the planned peak, and quick strides following a couple of easy runs each week to maintain your speed from Phase 1.

Run a few key races during Phase 2 to assess your fitness and accurately determine your goal marathon pace (or half-marathon pace, if you're training for a half-marathon).

Training Cycle 5: Aerobic Power and Acidosis Threshold (4 weeks)

The first training cycle of Phase 2 introduces acidosis threshold training while continuing with aerobic power (VO_2max), with one workout of each per week. The weekly mileage is 75% of the planned peak.

The acidosis threshold is an interesting physiological variable, demarcating the transition between running that is almost purely aerobic and running that includes significant anaerobic metabolism. Thus, the acidosis threshold discerns sustainable, metabolically balanced workloads from non-sustainable, non-metabolically balanced workloads. The speed at the acidosis threshold is the fastest speed that can be sustained exclusively by aerobic means. Raising your threshold enables you to run faster before you fatigue, because it enables you to run faster before anaerobic metabolism (and, consequently, the development of acidosis) begins to play a significant role. With training, what was once an anaerobic pace becomes high-end aerobic.

Since the development of metabolic acidosis begins when the lactate threshold is exceeded, I often refer to the threshold as the "acidosis threshold," as I do in the Endurance of Speed training program in this book, to take the emphasis off the innocuous lactate and place it on the fatigue-inducing acidosis, which is the physiological marker of interest.

The longer the race for which you're training, the more important the acidosis threshold becomes, because the more important it is to hold a faster aerobic pace for an extended period. The keys to success for marathon and half-marathon races are (1) getting your acidosis threshold pace as fast as possible and (2) being able to run as close to acidosis threshold pace as possible for as long as possible.

In comparison to VO_2max training, which is mostly about what's happening to your cardiovascular system, the site of adaptation of acidosis threshold training shifts from the cardiovascular system to the skeletal muscles. Acidosis threshold pace should feel comfortably hard, at the upper end of being purely aerobic. That comfortably hard feeling requires practice to attain and hold. When training for a marathon or half-marathon and working on specific endurance, it's almost always better to run workouts slower for a longer duration than to run faster for a shorter duration.

Acidosis threshold pace for recreational and intermediate-level runners:

- About 10-15 seconds per mile slower than 5K race pace
- Equal or very close to 10K race pace (if your 10K time is slower than about 50 minutes, threshold pace will be slightly faster than 10K race pace)
- 80-85% max heart rate

Acidosis threshold pace for competitive and highly trained runners:

- About 25-30 seconds per mile slower than 5K race pace
- About 15-20 seconds per mile slower than 10K race pace
- 85-90% max heart rate

Training Cycle 6: Aerobic Capacity & Acidosis Threshold (4 weeks)

The weekly mileage increases more drastically during Training Cycle 6, to 85-90% of the planned peak. The emphasis is on aerobic capacity (general endurance) and acidosis threshold (specific endurance), with two threshold workouts per week.

Training Cycles 7, 8, & 9: Aerobic Capacity/ Acidosis Threshold/Marathon Pace (4 weeks each)

Training Cycles 7, 8, and 9 emphasize acidosis threshold and marathon pace, with one workout of each per week, along with one long run each week. The weekly mileage continues to increase, reaching 100% of the planned peak in week 3 of Training Cycle 8, which you'll sustain for all four weeks of Training Cycle 9.

PHASE 3: TAPER
(2 weeks)

The training program concludes with the two-week taper of Training Cycle 10, during which you drastically back off on the volume of training to recover, with only 50% of your peak mileage during the first week and 30% of your peak mileage during the second week.

The goal of the taper is to recover from prior training without compromising your fitness. That's a delicate and individualistic balancing act. Your taper should be long enough that you're completely recovered from the training and are as fresh as possible for the race, but not so long that you start to lose fitness.

The specific workouts during the taper are of the same intensity but of a lesser volume (half to two-thirds the amount) than what you did during the specific preparation phase. The intensity will maintain fitness, while the reduced volume will enable you to recover.

The key to the taper is what preceded it, so make sure you run a significant amount of mileage during Phase 2 of the training program. Too many runners don't get as much from the taper because their weekly mileage is not that high. You can't taper down what hasn't been built up.

During the latter part of the taper, especially over the final few days before the race, increase the amount of carbohydrates in your diet to at least 80% of your daily calories, especially if you're preparing for a marathon. Like an airplane fueling up before its transcontinental flight, when you go to the start line of a marathon, your muscle and liver glycogen fuel tanks should be as full as possible.

PHASE 4: RECOVERY/TRANSITION
(2 weeks)

Following the training is a two-week recovery period of no running, if racing a marathon, or one week of no running and one week of light jogging and aerobic cross-training, if racing a half-marathon.

After running 26.2 miles as fast as you can, there is a considerable amount of muscle fiber damage that needs time to repair. Resist the urge to run for two weeks following the marathon.

It was getting later on the patio, where Sara and I were still talking about her training, the sun beginning its slow descent toward the horizon. She was nearly finished with her iced coffee, and the beads of water on the outside of the plastic cup had dried up.

"And that's how you become a faster marathon runner!" I exclaimed.

"Won't I get injured doing all that speed work?" she asked.

"That's a good question," I responded. "Many runners think the high intensity of running fast causes injuries, Sara, in part because that's what they are often told, but that's a myth. Research has shown that high-intensity running is not more injurious than is high-volume running.[34, 35]

"You can just as easily get injured running long distances slowly (with small muscular and ground reaction forces incurred tens of thousands of times) as you can running short distances fast (with large muscular and ground reaction forces incurred dozens of times); the difference is in the types of injuries the two training factors—high intensity and high volume—cause.

"To be more accurate, high intensity or high volume by themselves are seldom the cause of injury; it's the cumulative stress of high intensity or high volume that causes injuries due to inadequate recovery between high-intensity workouts and/or between high-mileage runs. You don't get injured by sprinting 100 meters ten times today. You get injured by sprinting 100 meters ten times today, then doing it again in forty-eight hours, then doing it again in forty-eight hours, and so on, since that doesn't give you enough time to recover and adapt between workouts."

"Okay, great. That makes sense," Sara said, sounding relieved. "But what about all the recommendations that runners should focus on aerobic endurance training to run a faster marathon?"

"Another good question. Don't misinterpret a speed-first approach with the neglect of endurance. The Endurance of Speed method does not neglect endurance. Quite the contrary. Indeed, if I were asked what's one thing that would make someone a better distance runner, I would say, 'Run more.' Of the many factors that impact a runner's performance, the weekly mileage has the biggest impact, whether he or she is training to race one mile or a marathon.

"The Endurance of Speed method includes plenty of aerobic endurance training, some of it hardcore, and even allows you to decide exactly how many miles to run per week based on percentages of your planned peak mileage. The major difference between the Endurance of Speed method and other methods is the initial development of speed before specific endurance.

"You see, Sara, your training program is a way of communicating the direction and progression of your training, how it intends to reach the end goal, and the specific benchmarks it will need to hit in order for it to work," I explained. "You must work *on* your training, not just *in* your training. Sometimes, you need to take a different approach, a different way to communicate the direction and progression of your training.

"When all the pieces of the training program are put together correctly and align with what you need to run faster, the entire training program should look like one fully integrated, beautifully designed system."

"How do I know that training this way will make me faster?" she asked.

"Because it works! It works because you planned it that way. Like an architect plans a house. An architect doesn't plan a house to crumble. An architect plans a house to stand firm. Your training program will stand firm and be successful because you planned it to be successful. Because you worked *on* it, not just *in* it. Because you understand what limits you now, and you understand how to raise that limit.

"The interval workouts, threshold runs, long runs, and marathon-pace runs are all parts. They mean little by themselves. You can't understand the value of a whole process by separating the parts from the process or the process from the parts. When you separate the parts from the process, there is no process. There are only parts. Parts without a process have no motion, no purpose. They're lifeless. Instead of being like fast running, filled with motion and purpose, it is the antithesis of fast running. To fully understand the role each part plays in the training program, you have to see it as part of the whole training program, not separate from the whole, by itself.

"Think about the long run you just did today before meeting me. That one run is a part. That one run, by itself, means nothing by itself. It is an integral, meaningful part of the entire training process that gives you meaning well beyond running a PR or qualifying for the Boston Marathon. When you remember the entire training process, you remember much more than any single run. You remember that the single run is part of a much larger process than enables you to narrow the gap between who you are and who you want to be."

Sara's eyes began to well up. She looked away for a moment, staring across the courtyard, seeming to want to say something, but she didn't.

"There is a process, Sara, filled with specific moving parts, to get you to that point, to enable you to achieve something with your running that transcends any single run. And, after all, isn't that where the joy of running and training comes from? To integrate the parts into the whole, so the whole becomes greater than the sum of its parts?

"That's what the training process is all about.

"And that successful training program will make you feel wonderful. You will be fast and powerful, with remarkable endurance that will enable you to sustain a much faster pace."

"That's what I want!" she exclaimed, nearly popping the lid off her iced coffee drink as she squeezed the cup in her hand.

"Excellent," I said, slapping the table. "Now, let's get to work."

THE ENDURANCE OF SPEED TRAINING PROGRAM

PHASE 1: GENERAL PREPARATION (16 WEEKS)

Training Cycle 1: Anaerobic Power (AP) (4 weeks)	
Week 1 55% peak mileage	3 Easy Runs 1 Long Run 2 AP Workouts (strides twice/week)
Week 2 55% peak mileage	3 Easy Runs 1 Long Run 2 AP Workouts (strides twice/week)
Week 3 55% peak mileage	3 Easy Runs 1 Long Run 2 AP Workouts (strides twice/week)
Week 4 (recovery) 35% peak mileage	4 Easy Runs 1 Long Run 1 AP Workout (strides twice/week)

Training Cycle 2: Anaerobic Capacity (AC) (4 weeks)	
Week 1 60% peak mileage	3 Easy Runs 1 Long Run 2 AC Workouts (strides twice/week)
Week 2 60% peak mileage	3 Easy Runs 1 Long Run 2 AC Workouts (strides twice/week)
Week 3 60% peak mileage	3 Easy Runs 1 Long Run 2 AC Workouts (strides twice/week)
Week 4 (recovery) 40% peak mileage	4 Easy Runs 1 Long Run 1 AC Workout (strides twice/week)

ENDURANCE OF SPEED TRAINING PROGRAM ◀ 65

Training Cycle 3: Anaerobic Capacity (AC) & Aerobic Power (VO$_2$max) (4 weeks)	
Week 1 65% peak mileage	3 Easy Runs 1 Long Run 1 AC Workout 1 VO$_2$max Workout (strides twice/week)
Week 2 65% peak mileage	3 Easy Runs 1 Long Run 1 AC Workout 1 VO$_2$max Workout (strides twice/week)
Week 3 65% peak mileage	3 Easy Runs 1 Long Run 1 AC Workout 1 VO$_2$max Workout (strides twice/week)
Week 4 (recovery) 45% peak mileage	4 Easy Runs 1 Long Run 1 AC Workout (strides twice/week)

Training Cycle 4: Aerobic Power (VO$_2$max) (4 weeks)	
Week 1 70% peak mileage	3 Easy Runs 1 Long Run 2 VO$_2$max Workouts (strides twice/week)
Week 2 70% peak mileage	3 Easy Runs 1 Long Run 2 VO$_2$max Workouts (strides twice/week)
Week 3 70% peak mileage	3 Easy Runs 1 Long Run 2 VO$_2$max Workouts (strides twice/week)
Week 4 (recovery) 50% peak mileage	4 Easy Runs 1 Long Run 1 VO$_2$max Workout (strides twice/week)

PHASE 2: SPECIFIC PREPARATION (20 WEEKS)

Training Cycle 5: Aerobic Power (VO$_2$max) & Acidosis Threshold (AT) (4 weeks)	
Week 1 75% peak mileage	3 Easy Runs 1 Long Run 1 VO$_2$max Workout 1 AT Workout (strides twice/week)
Week 2 75% peak mileage	3 Easy Runs 1 Long Run 1 VO$_2$max Workout 1 AT Workout (strides twice/week)
Week 3 75% peak mileage	3 Easy Runs 1 Long Run 1 VO$_2$max Workout 1 AT Workout (strides twice/week)
Week 4 (recovery) 55% peak mileage	4 Easy Runs 1 Long Run 1 VO$_2$max Workout (strides twice/week)

Training Cycle 6: Aerobic Capacity & Acidosis Threshold (AT) (4 weeks)	
Week 1 85% peak mileage	3 Easy Runs 1 Long Run 2 AT Workouts (strides twice/week)
Week 2 85% peak mileage	3 Easy Runs 1 Long Run 2 AT Workouts (strides twice/week)
Week 3 90% peak mileage	3 Easy Runs 1 Long Run 2 AT Workouts (strides twice/week)
Week 4 (recovery) 60% peak mileage	4 Easy Runs 1 Long Run 1 AT Workout (strides twice/week)

Training Cycle 7: Aerobic Capacity, Acidosis Threshold (AT), & Marathon Pace (MP) (4 weeks)

Week 1 90% peak mileage	3 Easy Runs 1 Long Run 1 AT Workout 1 MP Run (strides twice/week)
Week 2 90% peak mileage	3 Easy Runs 1 Long Run 1 AT Workout 1 MP Run (strides twice/week)
Week 3 95% peak mileage	3 Easy Runs 1 Long Run 1 AT Workout 1 MP Run (strides twice/week)
Week 4 (recovery) 65% peak mileage	4 Easy Runs 1 Long Run 1 AT Workout (strides twice/week)

Training Cycle 8: Aerobic Capacity, Acidosis Threshold (AT), & Marathon Pace (MP) (4 weeks)	
Week 1 95% peak mileage	3 Easy Runs 1 Long Run 1 AT Workout 1 MP Run (strides twice/week)
Week 2 95% peak mileage	3 Easy Runs 1 Long Run 1 AT Workout 1 MP Run (strides twice/week)
Week 3 100% peak mileage	3 Easy Runs 1 Long Run 1 AT Workout 1 MP Run (strides twice/week)
Week 4 (recovery) 70% peak mileage	4 Easy Runs 1 Long Run 1 AT Workout (strides twice/week)

Training Cycle 9: Aerobic Capacity, Acidosis Threshold (AT), & Marathon Pace (MP) (4 weeks)

Week 1 100% peak mileage	3 Easy Runs 1 Long Run 1 AT Workout 1 MP run (strides twice/week)
Week 2 100% peak mileage	3 Easy Runs 1 Long Run 1 AT Workout 1 MP Run (strides twice/week)
Week 3 100% peak mileage	3 Easy Runs 1 Long Run 1 AT Workout 1 MP Run (strides twice/week)
Week 4 100% peak mileage	3 Easy Runs 1 Long Run 1 AT Workout 1 MP Run (strides twice/week)

PHASE 3: TAPER
(2 WEEKS)

Training Cycle 10: Taper (2 weeks)	
Week 1 50% peak mileage	5 Easy Runs 1 AT Workout (strides twice/week)
Week 2 30% peak mileage	4 Easy Runs 1 AT Workout (strides twice/week) **Marathon or Half-Marathon Race**

PHASE 4: RECOVERY/TRANSITION
(2 WEEKS)

No running for 2 weeks (marathon) or one week (half-marathon). Light jogging/cross-training for second week.

Training Program Notes

> **Weekly Mileage:** Each week gives a recommendation for the percentage of peak mileage. Decide what your peak mileage will be for the 100% peak mileage weeks, and then follow the percentage recommendation for each week. For example, if you plan to run sixty miles per week as your peak weekly mileage, start the training program at 55% of that, which equals thirty-three miles for Week 1.

> **Long Runs:** Match the duration of the long runs (either by time or by mileage) to the percentage of peak weekly mileage. For example, if the week is at 70% of peak planned mileage, make the long run that week also 70% of the longest run you plan to do.

In Phase 2, as the long runs get very long, do some of your long runs without consuming carbohydrates to address their physiological purpose of depleting the muscle glycogen fuel tank, and do some while consuming carbohydrates to practice what you'll do in the marathon itself, using the same nutritional strategy (type of carbohydrates, timing, etc.) you'll use in the marathon.

> **Workouts:** For each week, select the specific workouts from the Endurance of Speed Workouts. For example, if the week says, "2 VO$_2$max Workouts," select two different VO$_2$max workouts from the Endurance of Speed Workouts. Spread the workouts far enough apart each week that you get enough recovery—at least two days.

Try different workout patterns to see which work best for you, such as Monday/Wednesday, Monday/Thursday, Tuesday/Friday, and so on. This is important in Phase 1 given the high intensity of the workouts, which may be accompanied by fatigue and muscle soreness if you're not used to this type of training, and in Phase 2 because of the volume of the workouts, which can cause a significant amount of leg fatigue.

If you're not used to very fast running, you may want to begin the training program with just one workout per week.

➢ **MP Runs:** Since MP runs are the most marathon-specific workouts you'll do, make sure you are ready for them by running gently the day or two before, and then take a rest day the day after. Run with others, if you can. Cap the distance you run at MP at eighteen miles, so you don't leave your marathon race in training.

As you get late into the program (Training Cycles 7-9), you don't have to do a long run every week along with a MP run, especially as the MP runs start to get long. Depending on how your legs feel, you can substitute the MP run for the long run, since the MP runs, although not quite as long as the easy-paced long runs, are more marathon-specific training.

If you're training for a half-marathon, run at goal half-marathon pace (HMP) for the MP runs instead of goal marathon pace, and cap the distance you run at HMP at nine miles. See the Endurance of Speed

ENDURANCE OF SPEED TRAINING PROGRAM ◀ 75

Workouts. For all MP runs, practice the same nutritional strategy (type of carbohydrates, timing, etc.) you'll use in the marathon.

> **Fatigue:** There is a normal amount of fatigue when training to run a faster marathon; you just need to determine how much fatigue is too much. Always listen to your body. If your legs are too fatigued, don't try to force all the workouts and long run into each week.

If two faster workouts and a long run are too much in one week, then take out one of the workouts. You can try alternating one workout one week with two workouts the following week. The training program is flexible, so play around with the combination of volume and intensity to figure out what is best for you.

> **Races:** I recommend including races in the Endurance of Speed Training Program, both to test your fitness at different stages and to keep you motivated throughout the training.

Run shorter races (1 mile to 5K) during the General Preparation Phase 1 and longer races (10K to half-marathon) during the Specific Preparation Phase 2. Try to plan your races at the end of Recovery Week 4 of each training cycle. If you run a race during Weeks 1, 2, or 3 of a training cycle, substitute the race for one of the workouts.

THE ENDURANCE OF SPEED WORKOUTS

Warm up for about 15 minutes before and cool down for about 10 minutes after workouts. For high-intensity workouts, like anaerobic power, anaerobic capacity, and VO_2max workouts, add a few 10-second quick strides at the end of the warm-up before starting the workouts. Your warm-up should start slowly and get progressively faster, so that the very end of the warm-up matches the speed you'll run in the workout, to create a smooth transition from the warm-up to the workout.

Strides

Controlled bursts of faster running for 10-30 seconds at about half-mile to 1-mile race effort following an easy run. Start with 3-4 reps and increase the number of reps throughout the training program, based on how your legs feel.

Aim for a fast, smooth feeling. Don't press to run fast. It should not feel like an interval workout. Relax, and focus on moving your legs quickly to increase stride rate and extending your legs behind you from your hip to increase stride length.

Run strides on flat ground with good footing. Take full recovery between each rep. Strides are neuromuscular, rather than metabolic, in nature. Taking too little recovery and/or making the strides last more than about 30 seconds introduces a metabolic demand, causes fatigue, and defeats the neuromuscular purpose of doing them.

Anaerobic Power (AP) Workouts

Sprint nearly as fast as you can, and walk for 3-5 minutes during recovery intervals.

AP Reps 1	10-second reps (or 50-75 meters) very fast, with 3-5 minutes' walk recovery, with as many reps as possible until very fatigued
AP Reps 2	100-meter reps very fast with 100-meter walk/jog recovery (if on a track, sprint 100-meter straightaways and walk/jog 100-meter curves), with as many reps as possible until very fatigued
AP Pyramid	1-2 sets of 5, 10, 15, 20, 15, 10, 5 seconds (or 25, 50, 75, 100, 75, 50, 25 meters) very fast with 3 minutes walk recovery and 10 minutes rest between sets

| AP Hills | 10- to 20-second very fast sprints up a short, steep hill (8-10% grade), with jog down recovery, with as many reps as possible until very fatigued |

Anaerobic Capacity (AC) Workouts

Run at half-mile to 1-mile race pace (about 30-45 seconds per mile faster than 5K pace). If you don't know how fast you can run a half-mile or 1 mile, just run fast, but leave a little in reserve so you can repeat the rep multiple times at the same pace. Jog during recovery intervals for double the amount of time spent running.

| AC Reps 1 | 20- to 40-second reps (or 100-200 meters) fast with 200-meter jog recovery, with as many reps as possible until very fatigued |

AC Reps 2	60- to 80-second reps (or 300-400 meters) @ 1-mile race pace with double time jog recovery, with as many reps as possible until very fatigued
AC Reps 3	2 sets of 30, 60, 30 seconds @ half-mile to 1-mile race pace with double time jog recovery between reps & 5 minutes standing/walking rest between sets
AC Ladder	2-4 sets of 30, 45, 60 seconds @ half-mile to 1-mile race pace with double time jog recovery between reps & 5 minutes standing/walking rest between sets
AC Pyramid	1-2 sets of 20, 40, 60, 80, 60, 40, 20 seconds (or 100, 200, 300, 400, 300, 200, 100 meters) @ half-mile to 1-mile race pace with double time jog recovery & 5 minutes standing/walking rest between sets

Aerobic Power (VO₂max) Workouts

Run at a pace that feels hard but manageable, with jogging recovery intervals equal to or slightly less than the time spent running.

Recreational and intermediate-level runners:
- 1.5-mile to 2-mile pace
- 20-25 seconds per mile faster than 5K pace
- 40-45 seconds per mile faster than 10K pace
- 95-100% max heart rate

Competitive and highly trained runners:
- Equal or very close to 2-mile/3K pace
- 10-15 seconds per mile faster than 5K pace
- 25-30 seconds per mile faster than 10K pace
- 95-100% max heart rate

VO₂max Long Reps	800, 1,000, or 1,200-meter reps @ VO₂max pace with equal time or slightly less than equal time jog recovery, with as many reps as possible until very fatigued
VO₂max Long Reps 2	Mile reps @ slightly slower than VO₂max pace (about 5K pace) with half time jog recovery, with as many reps as possible until very fatigued

VO$_2$max Short Reps	400-meter reps @ VO$_2$max pace with half time jog recovery, with as many reps as possible until very fatigued
VO$_2$max Short Reps2	200-meter reps @ slightly faster than VO$_2$max pace with 100-meter jog recovery, with as many reps as possible until very fatigued
VO$_2$max Ladder	2 sets of 800, 1,000, 1,200 meters @ VO$_2$max pace with equal time or slightly less than equal time jog recovery
VO$_2$max Cut-Down	1-2 sets of 1,600, 1,200, 1,000, 800, 400 meters @ slightly slower than VO$_2$max pace (about 5K pace) for 1,600; @ VO$_2$max pace for 1,200, 1,000, & 800; and slightly faster than VO$_2$max pace for 400, all with equal time or slightly less than equal time jog recovery
VO$_2$max Pyramid	1-2 sets of 800, 1,000, 1,200, 1,000, 800 meters @ VO$_2$max pace with equal time or slightly less than equal time jog recovery

Acidosis Threshold (AT) Workouts

Run at a pace that feels comfortably hard and at the upper end of being purely aerobic. Keep the pace as steady as possible, with little to no fluctuation.

Recreational and intermediate-level runners:
- 10-15 seconds per mile slower than 5K pace
- Equal or very close to 10K pace (if your 10K time is slower than about 50 minutes, pace will be slightly faster than 10K pace)
- 80-85% max heart rate

Competitive and highly trained runners:
- 25-30 seconds per mile slower than 5K pace
- 15-20 seconds per mile slower than 10K pace
- 85-90% max heart rate

AT Run	20-30 minutes @ AT pace
Long AT Run	40-70 minutes @ 10-20 seconds per mile (6-12 seconds per kilometer) slower than AT pace
Long AT Run 2	60-90 minutes, with first quarter @ easy pace, second quarter @ 10-20 seconds per mile (6-12 seconds per kilometer) slower than AT pace, third quarter @ AT pace, and

	fourth quarter @ faster than AT pace
AT Reps	Half-mile (800 meters) or mile reps @ AT pace with 1:00 slow walking rest, with as many reps as possible until very fatigued (try to run at least 12 reps if doing 800-meter reps or at least 5-6 reps if doing mile reps)
AT+ Reps	Half-mile (800 meters) or 1,000-meter reps @ 5-10 seconds per mile (3-6 seconds per kilometer) faster than AT pace, with 45 seconds rest between reps, with as many reps as possible until very fatigued (may be divided into sets of 4, with 2 minutes rest between sets)
Easy/AT Combo Run 1	3-4 miles @ AT pace + 8 miles easy

Easy/AT Combo Run 2	5 miles easy + 2-3 miles @ AT pace + 5 miles easy + 2-3 miles @ AT pace
Easy/AT Combo Run 3	10 miles easy + 3-4 miles @ AT pace

Marathon Pace (MP) & Half-Marathon Pace (HMP) Workouts

Run at your realistic goal marathon (or half-marathon) pace. Keep the pace as steady as possible, with little to no fluctuation.

MP 1	10-18 miles (or 70-125 minutes) @ MP, starting at the shorter end of the range and extending toward the longer end of the range (over months of training, not every week)
MP 2	10 miles easy + 8-10 miles @ MP
HMP 1	5-9 miles (or 35-65 minutes) @ HMP, starting at the shorter end of the range and extending toward the longer end of the range (over months of training, not every week)

HMP 2   7 miles easy + 3-5 miles @
                       HMP

Long Runs

Run at a pace that feels gentle, at which you can hold a conversation (70-75% max heart rate, or about 2 minutes per mile or 1:15 per kilometer slower than 5K pace), for 50-100% longer than easy runs.

Easy Runs

Run at a pace that feels gentle, at which you can hold a conversation (70-75% max heart rate, or about 2 minutes per mile or 1:15 per kilometer slower than 5K pace). Fill in easy runs into your week to meet your planned weekly mileage, but also remember to listen to your legs and run less if you need to, since these easy running days are important to recover from and adapt to the harder workouts.

COOL-DOWN

THE SUN WAS BEGINNING to set as Sara and I sat on the patio, pulling the temperature down with it. Our conversation was coming to an end. Sara knew it and I knew it.

I had shared with her nearly everything I wanted to share. All that was left was to tie the speed and endurance pieces together, for her to see how each piece is essential and how each essential piece fits within the bigger picture to create a systematic, progressive training program that will help her become a faster marathon runner. The marathon runner she wanted to become.

"Thank you, Jason, for taking the time to explain things to me, for helping me understand how and why to become a faster runner first, before working on my endurance," she said, seemingly satisfied with the new direction she was headed.

"It's been my pleasure, Sara. I am confident you will apply what you have learned. Oftentimes, runners' performances plateau not because of what they do, but because of what they don't do. And one of the things many runners don't do when they start running as adults is real speed work. They never become fast runners. But if you want something you've never had, you must do something you've never done."

Sara nodded. She didn't need to say anything. I knew she understood. She knew she had to work *on* her training, not just *in* her training. She knew she had to look at her training as a process full of parts, fulfilling each part of the process to first become as fast as she could, and then work on her endurance of speed.

One year later, that process worked for Sara. She ran her next marathon in 3:24, easily qualifying for the Boston Marathon and making her dream a reality.

ENDNOTES

[1] Jones, J.H. and Lindstedt, S.L. Limits to maximal performance. *Annual Review of Physiology*, 55:547-569, 1993.

[2] Lieberman, D.E., Warrener, A.G., Wang, J., and Castillo, E.R. Effects of stride frequency and foot position at landing on braking force, hip torque, impact peak force and the metabolic cost of running in humans. *Journal of Experimental Biology*, 218:3406-3414, 2015.

[3] Lombardo, M.P. and Deaner, R.O. You can't teach speed: sprinters falsify the deliberate practice model of expertise. *PeerJ*, 2:e445, 2014.

[4] Sinnett, A.M., Berg, K., Latin, R.W., and Noble, J.M. The relationship between field tests of anaerobic power and 10-km run performance. *Journal of Strength and Conditioning Research*, 15(4):405-412, 2001.

[5] Yamanaka, R., Ohnuma, H., Ando, R., Tanji, F., Ohya, T., Hagiwara, M., and Suzuki, Y. Sprinting ability as an important indicator of performance in elite long-distance runners. *International Journal of Sports Physiology and Performance*, 15:141-145, 2020.

[6] Tharp, L., Berg, K., Latin, R.W., and Stuberg, W. The relationship of aerobic and anaerobic power to distance running performance. *Sports Medicine, Training and Rehabilitation*, 7:215-225, 1997.

[7] Yamanaka, R., Ohnuma, H., Ando, R., Tanji, F., Ohya, T., Hagiwara, M., and Suzuki, Y. Sprinting ability as an important indicator of performance in elite long-distance runners. *International Journal of Sports Physiology and Performance*, 15:141-145, 2020.

[8] Sinnett, A.M., Berg, K., Latin, R.W., and Noble, J.M. The relationship between field tests of anaerobic power and 10-km run performance. *Journal of Strength and Conditioning Research*, 15(4):405-412, 2001.

[9] Pirie, G. *Running Wild*. London: W.H. Allen, 1961.

[10] Lydiard, A. and Gilmour, G. *Running the Lydiard Way*. Mountain View, CA: World Publishing, 1978.

[11] Noakes, T. *Lore of Running*. Champaign, IL: Human Kinetics, 1991.

[12] Noakes, T.D. Implications of exercise testing for prediction of athletic performance: a contemporary perspective. *Medicine and Science in Sports and Exercise*, 20(4):319-330, 1988.

[13] Ibid.

[14] Iaia, F.M. and Bangsbo, J. Speed endurance training is a powerful stimulus for physiological adaptations and performance improvements of athletes. *Scandinavian Journal of Medicine & Science in Sports*, 20(Suppl. 2):11-23, 2010.

[15] Skovgaard, C., Brandt, N., Pilegaard, H., and Bangsbo, J. Combined speed endurance and endurance exercise amplify the exercise-induced PGC-1α and PDK4 mRNA response in trained human muscle. *Physiological Reports*, 4(14):e12864, 2016.

[16] Prestes, J., De Lima, C., Frollini, A.B., Donatto, F.F., and Conte, M. Comparison of linear and reverse linear periodization effects on maximal strength and body composition. *Journal of Strength and Conditioning Research*, 23(1):266-274, 2009.

[17] Rhea, M.R., Phillips, W.T., Burkett, L.N., Stone, W.J., Ball, S.D., Alvar, B.A., and Thomas, A.B. A comparison of linear and daily undulating periodized programs with equated volume and intensity for local muscular endurance. *Journal of Strength and Conditioning Research*, 17(1):82-87, 2003.

[18] Bradbury, D.G., Landers, G.J., Benjanuvatra, N., and Goods, P.S. Comparison of linear and reverse linear periodized programs with equated volume and intensity for endurance running performance. *Journal of Strength and Conditioning Research*, 34(5):1345-1353, 2020.

[19] Arroyo-Toledo, J.J., Cantos-Polo, I., Liedtke, J., and Palomo-Vélez, J.C. Concentrated load on a reverse periodization, propel higher positives effects on track test performance, than traditional sequence. *Imperial Journal of Interdisciplinary Research*, 3(2):470-476, 2017.

[20] Gómez Martín, J.P., Clemente-Suárez, V.J., and Ramos-Campo, D.J. Hematological and running performance modification of trained athletes after reverse vs. block training periodization. *International Journal of Environmental Research and Public Health*, 17(13):4825, 2020.

[21] Clemente-Suárez, V.J. and Ramos-Campo, D.J. Effectiveness of reverse vs. traditional linear training periodization in triathlon. *International Journal of Environmental Research and Public Health*, 16(15):2807, 2019.

[22] Sylta, Ø., Tønnessen, E., Hammarström, D., Danielsen, J., Skovereng, K., Ravn, T., Rønnestad, B.R., Sandbakk, Ø., and Seiler, S. The effect of different high-intensity periodization models on endurance adaptations. *Medicine and Science in Sports and Exercise*, 48(11):2165-2174, 2016.

[23] Faina, M., Billat, V., Squadrone, R., De Angelis, M., Koralsztein, J.P., and Dal Monte, A. Anaerobic contribution to the time to exhaustion at the minimal exercise intensity at which maximal oxygen uptake occurs in elite cyclists, kayakists and swimmers. *European Journal of Applied Physiology*, 76:13-20, 1997.

[24] Sloth, M., Sloth, D., Overgaard, K., and Dalgas, U. Effects of sprint interval training on VO_2max and aerobic exercise performance: A systematic review and meta-analysis. *Scandinavian Journal of Medicine & Science in Sports*, 23(6):e341-e352, 2013.

[25] Billat, V. Current perspectives on performance improvement in the marathon: From universalisation to training optimisation. *New Studies in Athletics*, 20(3):21-39, 2005.

[26] Paavolainen, L., Hakkinen, K., Hamalainen, I., Nummela, A., and Rusko, H. Explosive-strength training improves 5-km running time by improving running economy and muscle power. *Journal of Applied Physiology*, 86(5):1527-1533, 1999.

[27] Spurrs, R.W., Murphy, A.J., and Watsford, M.L. The effect of plyometric training on distance running performance. *European Journal of Applied Physiology*, 89(1):1-7, 2003.

[28] Turner, A.M., Owings, M., and Schwane, J.A. Improvement in running economy after 6 weeks of plyometric training. *Journal of Strength and Conditioning Research*, 17(1):60-67, 2003.

[29] Berryman, N., Maurel, D.B., and Bosquet, L. Effect of plyometric vs. dynamic weight training on the energy cost of running. *Journal of Strength and Conditioning Research*, 24(7):1818-1825, 2010.

[30] Saunders, P.U., Telford, R.D., Pyne, D.B., Peltola, E.M., Cunningham, R.B., Gore, C.J., and Hawley, J.A. Short-term plyometric training improves running economy in highly trained middle and long distance runners. *Journal of Strength and Conditioning Research*, 20(4):947-954, 2006.

[31] Abernethy, P.J., Thayer, R., and Taylor, A.W. Acute and chronic responses of skeletal muscle to endurance and sprint exercise. A review. *Sports Medicine*, 10(6):365-389, 1990.

[32] Baden, D.A., McLean, T.L., Tucker, R., Noakes, T.D., and St. Clair Gibson, A. Effect of anticipation during unknown or unexpected exercise duration on rating of perceived exertion, affect, and physiological function. *British Journal of Sports Medicine*, 39:742-746, 2005.

[33] Tucker, R. and Noakes, T.D. The physiological regulation of pacing strategy during exercise: a critical review. *British Journal of Sports Medicine*, 43(6):e1, 2009.

[34] Ramskov, D., Rasmussen, S., Sørensen, H., Parner, E.T., Lind, M., and Nielsen, R. Progression in running intensity or running volume and the development of specific injuries in recreational runners: Run Clever, a randomized trial using competing risks. *Journal of Orthopaedic & Sports Physical Therapy*, 8(10):740-748, 2018.

[35] Ramskov, D., Rasmussen, S., Sørensen, H., Parner, E.T., Lind, M., and Nielsen, R.O. Run Clever – No difference in risk of injury when comparing progression in running volume and running intensity in recreational runners: A randomised trial. *BMJ Open Sport & Exercise Medicine*, 4(1):e000333, 2018.

ABOUT THE AUTHOR

THE PASSION JASON KARP found as a kid for the science of athletic performance started with a race around the track in sixth grade in Marlboro, New Jersey. Little did Jason know how much it would define his career and life. A Brooklyn, New York native, he grew up playing baseball and soccer and running track. His passion and curiosity placed him on a path that he still follows as a coach, exercise physiologist, author, speaker, and creator of the popular REVO$_2$LUTION RUNNING coaching certification program, which was acquired by International Sports Sciences Association (ISSA) in 2022.

Jason has given hundreds of international lectures and has been a featured speaker at the world's top fitness conferences and coaching clinics. He has also given a TEDx talk, *How Running Like an Animal Makes Us Human*. He has been an instructor for USA Track & Field's Level-3 coaching certification and for coaching camps at the U.S. Olympic Training Center.

At age twenty-four, he became one of the youngest college head coaches in the country, leading the Georgian Court University women's cross-country team to the regional championship and winning honors as NAIA Northeast Region Coach of the Year. While coaching high school track and field and cross country, he has produced state qualifiers and All-Americans. In 2021, he became the first American distance running coach to move to Kenya to coach a group of Kenyan runners.

A prolific writer, Jason has more than 400 publications in coaching and fitness trade and consumer magazines, is the author of thirteen other books, and is editor of the sixth edition of *Track & Field Omnibook*.

For his contributions to the industry, Jason was awarded the 2011 IDEA Personal Trainer of the Year (the fitness industry's highest award), is a two-time recipient of the President's Council on Sports, Fitness, & Nutrition Community Leadership Award (2014, 2019), and was a 2019 finalist for Personal Fitness Professional Trainer of the Year and 2020 finalist for Association of Fitness Studios Influencer of the Year.

Jason received his PhD in exercise physiology with a physiology minor from Indiana University, his MBA in entrepreneurship from San Diego State University, his master's degree in kinesiology from the University of Calgary, and his bachelor's degree in exercise and sport science with an English minor from Penn State University. His research has been published in several scientific journals, and he serves as a journal expert peer reviewer.